THE BACKWOODS OF CANADA

Catharine Parr Traill

*

The backwoods of Canada

*

*

*

Selections

Introduction: Clara Thomas

General Editor: Malcolm Ross

New Canadian Library No. 51

MCCLELLAND & STEWART LIMITED

© in
Canada by
McClelland and Stewart
Limited 1966

Introduction © McClelland
and Stewart Limited 1971

0-7710-9151-6

All rights reserved.
No part of this book may be reproduced in any form without permission in writing from the publishers, except by a reviewer who may quote brief passages in a review to be printed in a magazine or newspaper.

The Canadian Publishers
McClelland and Stewart
Limited
25 Hollinger Road,
Toronto

Printed and bound
in Canada

CONTENTS

*

INTRODUCTION

The publication of this selected edition of Catharine Parr Traill's *The Backwoods of Canada* in the New Canadian Library series completes a significant trilogy of feminine report on Canada in the nineteenth century. Mrs Moodie's *Roughing It in the Bush*, Mrs Jameson's *Winter Studies and Summer Rambles in Canada* and Mrs Traill's *Backwoods* together reveal a comprehensive composite picture taken from three widely ranging angles of vision.

In Mrs Traill's writing, sturdy adaptability to the emigrant's condition, acceptance of the present, and optimism for the future dominate:

> Canada is the land of hope; here everything is new; everything going forward; it is scarcely possible for arts, sciences, agriculture, manufactures to retrograde; they must keep advancing; though in some situations the progress may seem slow, in others they are proportionably rapid.

The style of her writing is unfailingly simple, clear, and factual; its matter-of-factness and lack of dramatic embellishment make *The Backwoods in Canada* an admirable monument to the purpose which Mrs Traill stated in her introduction:

> She prefers honestly representing facts in their real and true light, that the female part of the emigrant's family may be enabled to look them firmly in the face; to find a remedy in female ingenuity and expediency for some difficulties; and, by being properly prepared, encounter the rest with that high-spirited cheerfulness of which women under circumstances the most discouraging, often give extraordinary proofs.

Mrs Traill's book was designed as a handbook for emigrating gentlewomen; its authoress was well-suited, by nature and by training, to produce such a work. She was born in London, England, in 1802, the youngest of nine children of Thomas Strickland, a gentleman of means who moved his family in 1808 to Reydon Hall in Sussex and who took pleasure in encouraging and in superintending the education of his children. The vignettes of Strickland family living which have filtered through time are attractive and familiar ones—an articulate, literary, scribbling family, encouraged by their parents and by the resources of a sizable library to burrow after knowledge and to record their findings. Burneys, Austens, Martineaus, Mills, Murphys (Anna Jameson), Brontës (though sadly blighted)—across time all of these families reveal a similar pattern of indefatigable industry and enthusiasm for stretching minds, imaginations, and writing skills.

At least seven of the Strickland children became published authors: Elizabeth and Agnes were best known for their *Lives of the Queens of England*; Sara and Jane were devoted to far-flung historical horizons, the latter author of *Rome, Regal and Republican*; Susanna's *Roughing It in the Bush* is the best known of a very large literary output; Samuel, after firmly establishing himself in Upper Canada, wrote his account of pioneering, *Twenty-seven Years in Canada West*. Catharine, though the youngest, had been published first: she was the author of nine children's books before she came to Canada.

In 1832 she married Thomas Traill, a retired officer of the Royal Scottish Fusiliers. Immediately they set sail for Canada to take up the grant of land to which Mr Traill was entitled, their destination the Otonabee district of Upper Canada, near the present city of Peterborough. There Samuel Strickland had immigrated some years earlier and shortly afterward the Strickland family Odyssey was completed by the immigration to the same area of Susanna and her husband, Mr Moodie.

The letters which make up *The Backwoods of Canada*, except for four addressed to friends, were written by Catharine Traill to her mother from 1832 to 1835. They were published by Charles Knight in 1836 in his "Library of Entertaining Knowledge," Mrs Traill's introduction designating her particular audience as "the wives and daughters of emigrants of the higher class," her appendices a compendium of factual data ranging from instructions for the making of maple sugar to almanac information regarding numbers and dispersal of immigrants to the Canadas in the years 1829 to 1834. The letters themselves bear strong, if negative, evidence of editing: no extraneous family chit-chat, above all no emotional imbalance, disturb their calm and lucid gentility.

The record begins with the emigrants' departure from

Greenock in July of 1832; it provides a detailed account of their voyage, of their introduction to Canada—and to the cholera, and of their journey to the "interior" where they stayed with brother Samuel near Peterborough until October, when a log-house was ready on their own land. Thereafter the story is one of challenges met and overcome, with a precision of detail provided for others who will follow to find similar conditions, and a substantial assurance of qualified success for those whose hopes are based on reality, industry, and what Mrs Traill would call "sound domestic economy."

Every line evidences the maturity and commonsense of the author; such a book might have been written by Elizabeth Bennet if, already tempered in Jane Austen's furnace, she and Mr Darcy had deemed emigration necessary for the future of their family fortunes. Catharine Traill was sustained by firmer and far more positive considerations than a naïve optimism would provide. She had a healthy respect for property and a strong sense of family position and solidarity:

> Children should be taught to appreciate the devoted love that has induced their parents to overcome the natural reluctance felt by all persons to quit forever the land of their forefathers . . . that their children may be placed in a situation in which, by industry and activity, the substantial comforts of life may be permanently obtained, and a landed property handed down to them and their children after them.

She walked easily with the conventions of her class and time —allegiance to the Crown and its representatives, a distrust of all things "republican" and American. Her most emotional prose, though still conventionally rhetorical, denounces the Mackenzie rebellion in letters written later than the *Backwoods* collection:

> Mackenzie raised the cry of rebellion, and the answer has been the rallying of thousands and tens of thousands of valiant men round the standard of their young Queen—with the thrilling cry echoed from lake to lake and forest to plains "Long live Victoria and the British Constitution."

Conventional pieties do not impinge upon the reader, but the impression of religious faith is strong, as is the impression of an independent spirit recording with knowledgeable appreciation the advantages which accrue to her new position:

> I was too much inclined to spurn with impatience the fetters that etiquette and fashion are wont to impose on society till they rob its followers of all freedom and independence of will. . . . And I must freely confess to you that I do prize and enjoy my present liberty in this country exceedingly: in this we possess the advantage over you.

Catharine Traill found in Canadian nature the sustaining and compensating substitute for all those niceties of polite civilization for which many emigrant women mourned hopelessly. She had the priceless sense of wonder at both the magnificence and the precision of nature which has been the most excellently communicated quality of Canada's artists and poets. Sometimes she described the grandeur of a scene with an apt, but conventionally romantic, technique:

> I have stood of a bright winter day looking with infinite delight on the beautiful mimic waterfalls congealed into solid ice along the bank of the river; and by the mill-dam, from contemplating these pretty frolics of Father Frost, I have been led to picture to myself the sublime scenery of the Arctic regions.

Always, however, the individual and the precise in nature called forth all the curiosity and delicacy of observation, the skill and elegance of description of the knowledgeable botanist. Catharine Traill had been an enthusiastic amateur in botany since girlhood; in Canada she found unlimited scope for her interests and for her self-training. Her *Canadian Wild Flowers* (1868) and *Studies in Plant Life in Canada* (1885) are classic records of nineteenth-century Canadian flora and the climactic works of her writing career; they brought her fame as a distinguished naturalist, an encouraging gift of £100 from the British government, and in 1893 an island in the river Otonabee, an acknowledgement of her work by the Canadian government.

The Backwoods of Canada gives early and ample evidence of Mrs Traill's propensity. In two paragraphs she disposes of her attack of cholera, the most dreaded epidemic of the 30's and a plague that killed thousands of immigrants; some eighteen pages are required, however, to record with the precision of the scientist and the fresh delight of the discoverer the wild-flowers she finds around her new home:

> I have promised to collect some of the most singular of our native flowers for one of the Professors of Botany in the Edinburgh University. . . . A very beautiful plant of the lily tribe abounds both in our woods and clearings . . . the flower is either deep red, or of a dazzling white, though the latter is often found stained with a delicate blush-pink, or a deep green; the latter appears to be caused by the calix running into the petal . . . the flower consists of three petals, the calix three; it belongs to the class and order *Hexandria monogynia*; style, three-cleft; seed-vessel of three valves.

Something of the same precise expression of observation is evident in her descriptions of the Indians living in the Peterborough district. To them she brought a warm curiosity and the acceptance of a way of life utterly alien to her, but one which she depicted with a keen eye for its colour, a full realization of its transience, and notably without emotional case-making. This section of *The Backwoods of Canada* was part of a lengthy excerpt used by Mr N. P. Willis in the text of *Canadian Scenery*, the *de luxe* publication of 1842, illustrated by the many drawings of W. H. Bartlett.

Catharine Parr Traill wrote seventeen books, eight of them after coming to Canada, and, in addition, many occasional pieces—she was, for example, a frequent contributor to John Lovell's Montreal publication, *The Literary Garland*. She and her husband had a family of nine children, a conspicuous contribution of the kind of settler nineteenth-century Canada most needed. She died in her ninety-eighth year, her naturalist's interest alert to the very end of her life.

Her most popular book for children was called, fittingly, *Canadian Crusoes* (1853). There was much of Crusoe in Catharine Traill: her mind was rational, empiric, and scientific in its bent and her writing talents were best employed when she recorded her observing and experiencing of her new environment. *The Backwoods of Canada* provides none of the histrionics which are so much a part of the writing of Susanna Moodie or of Anna Jameson; it gives us instead a portrait and a record of the woman Catharine Parr Traill was and wished to be—a pioneer gentlewoman, superbly equipped for her rôle, eminently successful in it, and notably fitted for the advising of others who would follow in her path.

CLARA THOMAS

York University,
Toronto,
February, 1965.

CHAPTER 1 *The Ocean Voyage*

Brig *Laurel*, July 18, 1832.

I received your last kind letter, my dearest mother, only a few hours before we set sail from Greenock. As you express a wish that I should give you a minute detail of our voyage, I shall take up my subject from the time of our embarkation, and write as inclination prompts me. Instead of having reason to complain of short letters, you will, I fear, find mine only too prolix.

After many delays and disappointments, we succeeded at last in obtaining a passage in a fast-sailing brig, the *Laurel*, of Greenock; and favourable winds are now rapidly carrying us across the Atlantic.

The *Laurel* is not a regular passenger-ship, which I consider an advantage, for what we lose in amusement and variety we assuredly gain in comfort. The cabin is neatly fitted up, and I enjoy the luxury (for such it is, compared with the narrow berths of the state cabin) of a handsome sofa, with crimson draperies, in the great cabin. The state cabin is also ours. We paid fifteen pounds each for our passage to Montreal. This was high, but it includes every expense; and, in fact, we had no choice. The only vessel in the river bound for Canada was a passenger-ship, literally swarming with emigrants, chiefly of the lower class of Highlanders.

The only passengers besides ourselves in the *Laurel* are the captain's nephew, a pretty yellow-haired lad, about fifteen years of age, who works his passage out, and a young gentleman who is going out as clerk in a merchant's house in Quebec. He seems too much wrapped up in his own affairs to be very communicative to others.

I was much pleased with the scenery of the Clyde; the day we set sail was a lovely one, and I remained on deck till nightfall. The morning light found our vessel dashing gallantly along, with a favourable breeze, through the North Channel; that day we saw the last of the Hebrides, and before night lost sight of the north coast of Ireland. A wide expanse of water and sky is now our only prospect, unvaried by any object save the distant and scarcely to be traced outline of some vessel just seen at the verge of the horizon, a speck in the immensity of space, or sometimes a few sea-fowl. I love to watch these wanderers of the ocean as they rise and fall with the rocking billows or flit about our vessel; and often I wonder whence they came, to what distant shore they are bound, and if they make the rude wave their home and resting-place during the long day and dark night; and then I recall to mind the words of the American poet, Bryant,

He who from zone to zone
Guides through the boundless air their certain flight,
In the long way that I must tread alone
Will guide my steps aright.

Though we have been little more than a week on board, I am getting weary of the voyage. I can only compare the monotony of it to being weather-bound in some country inn. I have already made myself acquainted with all the books worth reading in the ship's library; unfortunately, it is chiefly made up with old novels and musty romances.

I have endured the horrors of *mal de mer*, and except when the weather is fine I sit on a bench on the deck, wrapped in my cloak, and sew, or pace the deck with my husband, and talk over plans for the future, which in all probability will never be realized. I really do pity men who are not actively employed: women have always their needle as a resource against the overwhelming weariness of an idle life; but where a man is confined to a small space, such as the deck and cabin of a trading vessel, with nothing to see, nothing to hear, nothing to do, and nothing to read, he is really a very pitiable creature. Every space is utilized in a ship. The bench on which the bed of cloaks is spread for me covers the hen coop. Poor prisoners to be killed and cooked as needed!

There is one passenger on board that seems perfectly happy, if one may judge from the liveliness of the songs with which he greets us whenever we approach his cage. It is "Harry," the captain's goldfinch—"the *captain's mate*," as the sailors term him. This pretty creature has made no fewer than twelve voyages in the *Laurel*. "It is all one to him whether his cage is at sea or on land, he is still at home," said the captain, regarding his little favourite with an air of great affection.

I have already formed a friendship with the little captive. He never fails to greet my approach with one of his sweetest songs, and will take from my fingers a bit of biscuit, which he holds in his claws till he has thanked me with a few of his clearest notes. This mark of acknowledgement is termed by the steward, "saying grace." But his master views my attentions to his beloved "Harry" with a jealous eye. He has neither wife nor child to love him; he says, "I cannot afford to lose the least bit of Harry's love. I want it all."

The bird has no mate. It made twelve voyages to and fro to the West Indies with him.

If the wind still continues to favour us, the captain tells us we shall be on the banks of Newfoundland in another week. Farewell for the present.

CHAPTER 2 *Majestic and Mighty River*

Brig *Laurel*, River St Laurence,
August 6, 1832.

. . . We came within sight of the shores of Newfoundland on the 5th of August, just one month from the day we took our last look of the British Isles. Yet though the coast was brown, and rugged, and desolate, I hailed its appearance with rapture. Never did anything seem so refreshing and delicious to me as the land breeze that came to us bearing health and gladness on its wings. I had become very weak but soon revived as I felt the air from the land reaching us and some winged insects came to us—a welcome sight.

I had noticed with some curiosity the restless activity of the captain's bird some hours previous to "land" being proclaimed from the look-out station. He sang continually, and his note was longer, clearer, and more thrilling than heretofore; the little creature, the captain assured me, was conscious of the difference in the air as we approached the land. "I trust almost as much to my bird as to my glass," he said.

Our progress was somewhat tedious after we entered the gulf.

Ninety miles across is the entrance of this majestic river; it seems an ocean in itself. Half our time is spent poring over the great chart in the cabin, which is constantly being rolled and unrolled by my husband to gratify my desire of learning the names of the distant shores and islands which we pass.

We are without a pilot yet, and the captain being a cautious seaman is unwilling to risk the vessel on this dangerous navigation; so that we proceed but slowly on our voyage.

August 7—We were visited this morning by a beautiful little bird, not much larger than our gold-crested wren. I hailed it as a bird of good omen—a little messenger sent to bid us welcome to the New World, and I felt almost a childish joy at the sight of our little visitor. There are happy moments in our lives when we draw the greatest pleasure from the most trifling sources, as children are pleased with the most simple toy.

From the hour we entered the gulf a perceptible change had taken place in all on board. The captain, a man of grave, quiet manners, grew quite talkative. My husband was more than usually animated, and even the thoughtful young Scotchman became positively an entertaining person. The crew displayed the most lively zeal in the performance of their duty, and the goldfinch sang cheerily from dawn till sunset. As for me, hope was busy in my heart, chasing from it all feelings of doubt or regret that might sadden the present or cloud the future.

I am now able to trace distinctly the outline of the coast on the southern side of the river. Sometimes the high lands are suddenly enveloped in dense clouds of mist, which are in constant motion, rolling along in shadowy billows, now tinted with rosy light, now white and fleecy, or bright as silver, as they catch the sunbeams. So rapid are the changes that take place on this fog-bank that perhaps the next time I raise my eyes I behold the scene changed as if by magic. The misty curtain is slowly drawn up, as if by invisible hands, and the wild, wooded mountains partially revealed, with their bold, rocky shores and sweeping bays. At other times the vapoury volume, dividing, moves along the valleys and deep ravines like lofty pillars of smoke, or hangs in snowy draperies among the dark forest pines.

I am never weary of watching these fantastic clouds; they recall to me the pleasant time I spent in the Highlands among the cloud-capped hills of the north.

As yet, the air is cold, and we experience frequent squalls of wind and hail, with occasional peals of thunder; then again all is serene and bright, and the air is filled with fragrance, and flies and bees and birds come flitting past us from the shore.

August 8—Though I cannot but dwell with feelings of wonder and admiration on the majesty and power of this mighty river, I begin to grow weary of its immensity, and long for a nearer view of the shore; but at present we see nothing more than long lines of pine-clad hills, with here and there white specks, which they tell me are settlements and villages to the south; while huge mountains divested of verdure bound our view on the north side of the river. My admiration of mountainous scenery makes me dwell with more interest on that side of the river, and I watch the progress of cultivation among these rugged and inhospitable regions with positive pleasure.

During the last two days we have been anxiously looking out for a pilot to take us up to Quebec. Various signals have been fired, but hitherto without success; no pilot has condescended to visit us, so we are somewhat in the condition of a stage without a coachman, with only some inexperienced hand to hold the reins. I already perceive some manifestations of impatience appearing among us, but no one blames the captain, who is very anxious about the matter, as the river is full of rocks and shoals, and presents many difficulties to a person not intimately acquainted with the navigation. Besides, he is answerable for the safety of the ship to the underwriters in case he neglects to take a pilot on board.

* * *

While writing the above I was roused by a bustle on deck, and going up to learn the cause was informed that a boat with the long looked-for pilot had put off from the shore; but, after all the fuss and bustle, it proved only a French fisherman, with a poor ragged lad, his assistant. The captain with very little difficulty persuaded Monsieur Paul Breton to pilot us as far as Green Island, a distance of some hundred miles higher up the river, where he assured us we should meet with a regular pilot, if not before.

I have some little difficulty in understanding Monsieur Paul, as he speaks a peculiar patois; but he seems good-natured and obliging enough. He tells us the wheat is yet green, hardly in ear, and the summer fruits not yet ripe; but he says that at Quebec we shall find apples and fruit in plenty.

As we advance higher up the river, the country on both sides begins to assume a more genial aspect. Patches of verdure, with white cottages, are seen on the shores and scattered along the sides of the mountains; while here and there a village church rears its simple spire, distinguished above the surrounding buildings by its glittering vane and bright roof of tin. The southern shores are more populous but less picturesque than those of the north, but there is enough on either side to delight the eye.

This morning we anchored off the Isle of Bic, a pretty, low island, covered with trees and looking very pleasant. I felt a longing desire to set my foot on Canadian ground, and must own I was a little disappointed when the captain advised me to remain on board, and not attempt to make one of the party that were preparing to go on shore: my husband seconded the captain's wish, so I contented myself with leaning over the ship's side and feasting my eyes on the rich masses of foliage as they waved to and fro with the slight breeze that agitated them. I soon had reason to be thankful that I had not followed my own wayward will, for the afternoon proved foggy, and on the return of the boat I learned that the ground was swampy just where the party landed, and that they sank over their ankles in water. They reported the island to be covered knee-deep with a most luxuriant growth of white clover, tall trees, low shrubs, and an abundance of wild flowers.

That I might not regret not accompanying him, my husband brought me a delightful bouquet which he had selected for me. Among the flowers were fragrant red roses, *rosa lucida*, resembling those we call Scotch burnt-leaved, with smooth shining leaves and few if any thorns; the blue flower, Pulmonaria or Lungwort, which I had gathered in the Highlands; a pea with red blossoms and wreaths of lovely pale green foliage; a white fringed orchis, the smell of which was quite delicious. Besides these were several small white and yellow loosestrife flowers, and others with which I was totally unacquainted. The steward furnished me with a china jar and fresh water, so that I shall have the pleasure of a bouquet during the rest of the voyage. The sailors had not forgotten a green bough or two to adorn the ship, and the bird-cage was soon as bowery as leaves could make it. . . .

August 16—We reached Grosse Isle yesterday evening. It is a beautiful rocky island, covered with groves of beech, birch, ash, and fir trees. There are several vessels lying at anchor close to the shore; one bears the melancholy symbol of disease, the yellow flag; she is a passenger-ship, and has the smallpox and measles among her crew. When any infectious complaint appears on board, the yellow flag is hoisted, and the invalids conveyed to the cholera-hospital, a wooden building that had been erected on a rising bank above the shore. It is surrounded with palisadoes and a guard of soldiers.

There is also a temporary fort at some distance from the hospital, containing a garrison of soldiers, who are there to enforce the quarantine rules. These rules are considered as very defective, and in some respects quite absurd, and are productive of many severe evils to the unfortunate emigrants.

When the passengers and crew of a vessel do not exceed a certain number, they are not allowed to land, under a penalty both to the captain and to the offender; but if, on the contrary, they should exceed the stated number, *ill* or *well*, passengers and crew must all turn out and go on shore, taking with them their bedding and clothes, which are all spread out on the shore, to be washed, aired, and fumigated, giving the healthy every chance of taking the infection from the invalids near them. The sheds and buildings put up for the accommodation of those who are obliged to submit to the quarantine laws are in the same area as the hospital.

Nothing can exceed the longing desire I feel to be allowed to land and explore this picturesque island; the weather is so fine and the waving groves so green; the little rocky bays and inlets of the island appear so tempting; but to all my entreaties the visiting surgeon who came on board returned a decided negative.

A few hours after his visit, however, an Indian basket, containing strawberries and raspberries, with a large bunch of wild flowers, was sent on board for me with the surgeon's compliments.

I amuse myself with making little sketches of the surrounding scenery, or watching the groups of emigrants on shore. We have already seen the landing of the passengers of three emigrant ships. You may imagine yourself looking on a fair or crowded market, clothes waving in the wind or spread out on the earth, chests, bundles, baskets, men, women, and children, asleep or basking in the sun, some in motion busied with their goods, the women employed in washing or cooking in the open air beside the wood fires on the beach; while parties of children are pursuing each other in wanton glee, rejoicing in their newly-acquired liberty. Mixed with these you see the stately form and gay trappings of the sentinels, while the thin blue smoke of the wood fires, rising above the trees, heightens the picture and gives it an additional effect. On my husband remarking the picturesque appearance of the scene before us to one of the officers from the fort who had come on board, he smiled sadly, and replied, "Believe me, in this instance, as in many others, 'tis distance lends enchantment to the view. Could you take a nearer survey of some of those very picturesque groups which you admire, I think you would turn away from them with heart-sickness; you would there behold every variety of disease, vice, poverty, filth, and famine—human misery in its most disgusting and saddening forms; such pictures as Hogarth's pencil only could have portrayed, or Crabbe's pen described."

I petitioned the health officer's permission to go on shore at a wild spot far from the quarantine ground, but he was inexorable. I pleaded: "There is no one there; it will do no harm." "You think so, Madam, but you might see a redcoat with a bayonet among those green bushes to warn you off," he said with a grim smile. I was silenced.

August 17— . . . At ten last night, August the 16th, the lights of the city of Quebec were seen gleaming through the distance like a coronet of stars above the waters. At half-past ten we dropped anchor opposite the fort, and I fell asleep dreaming of the various scenes through which I had passed. Again I was destined to be disappointed in my expectations of going on shore. Pity my disappointment! The captain promised us a treat of new milk, white bread, and fruit. Alas! it was not to be. The words came to my mind, and only too true they proved:

> The best laid schemes of mice and men
> Gang aft agley.

Our fine play was never acted out. The visiting surgeon advised my husband by no means to land, as the mortality that still raged in the town made it very hazardous. He gave a melancholy description of the place. "Desolation and woe and great mourning—Rachel weeping for her children because they are not," are words that may well be applied to this city of the pestilence.

Nothing can be more imposing than the situation of Quebec, built on the sides and summit of a magnificent rock, on the highest point of which (Cape Diamond) stands the fortress overlooking the river, and commanding a most superb view of the surrounding scenes. I did, indeed, regret the loss of this noble prospect, the equal of which I suppose I shall never see. It would have been something to have thought on and recalled in after years, when buried in the solitude of the Canadian woods.

The opposite heights, being the Point Levis side, are highly picturesque, though less imposing than the rock on which the town stands. The bank is rocky, precipitous, and clothed with trees that sweep down to the water's edge, excepting where they are cleared away to give place to white cottages, gardens, and hanging orchards. But, in my opinion, much less is done with this romantic situation than might be effected if good taste were exercised in the buildings, and on the disposal of the ground. How lovely would such a spot be rendered in England or Scotland! Nature here has done all, and man but little, excepting sticking up some ugly wooden cottages, as mean as they are tasteless. It is, however, very possible there may be pretty villas and houses higher up, that are concealed from the eye by the intervening groves.

The river is considered to be just a mile across from Point Levis to the landing-stairs below the custom-house in Quebec; and it was a source of amusement to me to watch the horse ferry-boats that ply between the two shores. The captain told me there were not less than twelve of these comical-looking machines. They each have their regular hours, so that you see a constant succession going or returning. They carry a strange assortment of passengers: well- and ill-dressed; old and young; rich and poor; cows, sheep, horses, pigs, dogs, fowls, market-baskets, vegetables, fruit, hay, corn, anything and everything you will see by turns.

The boat is flat, railed round, with a wicket at each end to admit the live and dead stock that go out or are taken on board; the centre of the boat (if such it can be called) is occupied by four lean, ill-favoured hacks, who walk round and round, as if in a threshing machine, and work the paddles at each side. There is a sort of pen for the cattle.

I am told there is a monument erecting in honour of Wolfe, in the Governor's garden, looking towards the St Laurence, and to be seen from Point Levis; the inscription has not yet been decided upon.

The captain has just returned from the town. He very kindly brought on board a basket of ripe apples for me, besides fresh meat, vegetables, bread, butter, and milk. The deck is all bustle with custom-house officers, and men unloading a part of the ship's freight, which consists chiefly of rum, brandy, sugar, and coals, for ballast. We are to leave Quebec by five o'clock this evening. The *British America*, a superb steam-vessel of three decks, takes us in tow as far an Montreal. I must now say farewell.

CHAPTER 3 *Up River to Montreal*

Brig *Laurel*, St Laurence, below Montreal,
August 17, 1832.

. . . I was anxious to obtain a near view of a log-house or a shanty, and was somewhat disappointed in the few buildings of this kind that I saw along the banks of the river. It was not the rudeness of the material so much as the barn-like form of the buildings of this kind, and the little attention that was paid to the picturesque, that displeased me. In Britain even the peasant has a taste enough to plant a few roses or honeysuckles about his door or his casement, and there is the little bit of garden enclosed and neatly kept; but here no such attempt is made to ornament the cottages. We saw no smiling orchard or grove to conceal the bare log walls; and as to the little farm-houses, they are uglier still, and look so pert and ungraceful stuck upon the bank close to the water's edge.

Farther back a different style of building and cultivation appears. The farms and frame-houses are really handsome places, and in good taste, with clumps of trees here and there to break the monotony of the clearing. The land is nearly one unbroken level plain, apparently fertile and well farmed, but too flat for fine scenery. To my unpractised eye the dead level extent of country gave me the idea that all that wide space of land had once been a vast lake, and the few elevated spots islands on the surface. The country between Quebec and Montreal has all the appearance of having been under a long state of cultivation, especially on the right bank of the river. Still there is a great portion of forest standing which it will take years of labour to remove.

We passed some little grassy islands on which there were many herds of cattle feeding. I was puzzling myself to know how they got there, when the captain told me it was usual for farmers to convey their stock to these island pastures in flat-bottomed boats, or to swim them, if the place was fordable, and leave them to graze as long as the food continued good. If cows are put on an island within a reasonable distance of the farm, some person goes daily in a canoe to milk them. While he was telling me this, a log-canoe with a boy and a stout lass with tin pails paddled across from the bank of the river and proceeded to call together their herd.

We noticed some very pleasant rural villages to the right as we advanced, but our pilot was stupid, and could not, or would not, tell their names. It was Sunday morning, and we could just hear the quick tinkling of the church bells, and distinguish long lines of calèches, light waggons, with equestrians and pedestrians hastening along the avenue of trees that led to the churchyard; besides these, were boats and canoes crossing the river, bound to the same peaceful haven.

In a part of the St Laurence, where the channel is rendered difficult by shoals and sand-banks, there occur little lighthouses, looking somewhat like miniature watermills, on wooden posts, raised above the flat banks on which they are built. These droll little huts were inhabited, and we noticed a merry party, in their holiday clothes, enjoying a gossip with a party in a canoe below them. They looked clean and smart, and cheerful enough, but I did not envy them their situation, which I should think far from healthy.

Some miles below Montreal the appearance of the country became richer, more civilized, and populous; while the distant line of blue mountains, at the verge of the horizon, added an interest to the landscape. The rich tint of ripened harvest formed a beautiful contrast with the azure sky and waters of the St Laurence. The scenery of the river near Montreal is of a very different character to that below Quebec; the latter possesses a wild and rugged aspect, and its productions are evidently those of a colder and less happy climate. What the former loses in grandeur and picturesque effect, it gains in fertility of soil and warmth of temperature. In the lower division of the Province you feel that the industry of the inhabitants is forcing a churlish soil for bread; while in the upper, the land seems willing to yield her increase to a moderate exertion. Remember, these are merely the cursory remarks of a passing traveller, and founded on no personal experience.

There was a feeling of anxiety and dread upon our minds that we would hardly acknowledge to each other as we drew near to the city of the pestilence, as if ashamed of confessing a weakness that was felt; but no one spoke on the subject. With what unmixed delight and admiration at any other time should we have gazed on the scene that opened upon us.

The river here expands into a fine extensive lakelike basin, diversified with islands, on the largest of which Montreal is situated.

The lofty hill from which the town takes its name rises like a crown above it, and forms a singular and magnificent feature in the landscape, reminding me of some of the detached hills in the vicinity of Inverness.

Opposite to the Quebec suburbs [sic], just in front of the rapids, is situated the island of St Helen's, a spot of infinite loveliness. The centre of it is occupied by a grove of lofty trees, while the banks, sloping down to the water, seem of the most verdant turf. The scene was heightened by the appearance of the troops which garrison the island. The white tents and gay scarlet coats of the soldiers enlivened the scene.

The shores of the river, studded with richly cultivated farms; the village of Laprairie, with the little island of St Anne's in the distance; the glittering steeples and roofs of the city, with its gardens and villas, looked lovely by the softened glow of a Canadian summer sunset.

The church bells ringing for evening prayer, with the hum of voices from the shore, mingled not inharmoniously with the rush of the rapids.

These rapids are caused by a descent in the bed of the river. In some places this declination is gradual, in others sudden and abrupt. Where the current is broken by masses of limestone or granite rock, as at the Cascades, the Cedars, and the Long Sault, it creates whirlpools and cataracts. But the rapids below Montreal are not of this magnificent character, being made perceptible only by the unusual swiftness of the water, and its surface being disturbed by foam and waving lines and dimples. In short, I was disappointed in my expectation of seeing something very grand, and was half angry at these prettily behaved quiet rapids, to the foot of which we were towed in good style by our faithful consort the *British America*.

As the captain is uncertain how long he may be detained at Montreal, I shall send this letter without further delay, and write again as soon as possible.

CHAPTER 4 *Impressions of City and Country*

Nelson Hotel, Montreal, August 21.

. . . I was greatly disappointed in my first acquaintance with the interior of Montreal; a place of which travellers had said so much. I could compare it only to the fruits of the Dead Sea, which are said to be fair and tempting to look upon, but yield only ashes and bitterness when tasted by the thirsty traveller.

I noticed one peculiar feature in the buildings along the suburb facing the river—that they were mostly furnished with broad wooden balconies from the lower to the upper story; in some instances they surrounded the houses on three sides, and seemed to form a sort of outer chamber. Some of these balconies were ascended by flights of broad stairs from the outside.

I remember, when a child, dreaming of houses so constructed, and fancying them very delightful; and so I think they might be rendered, if shaded by climbing shrubs and adorned with flowers, to represent a hanging-garden or sweet-scented bowery walk. But nothing of this kind gladdened our eyes as we toiled along the hot streets. Every house of public resort was crowded from the top to the bottom with emigrants of all ages, English, Irish, and Scotch. The sounds of riotous merriment that burst from them seemed but ill assorted with the haggard, care-worn faces of many of the thoughtless revellers.

The contrast was only too apparent and too painful a subject to those that looked upon this show of outward gaiety and inward misery.

The cholera had made awful ravages, and its devastating effects were to be seen in the darkened dwellings and the mourning habiliments of all classes. An expression of dejection and anxiety appeared in the faces of the few persons we encountered in our walk to the hotel, which plainly indicated the state of their minds.

In some situations whole streets had been nearly depopulated; those that were able fled panic-stricken to the country villages, while others remained to die in the bosom of their families.

To no class, I am told, has the disease proved so fatal as to the poorer sort of emigrants. Many of these, debilitated by the privations and fatigue of a long voyage, on reaching Quebec or Montreal indulged in every sort of excess, especially the dangerous one of intoxication; and, as if purposely paving the way to certain destruction, they fell immediate victims to the complaint.

In one house eleven persons died, in aother seventeen; a little child of seven years old was the only creature left to tell the woeful tale. This poor desolate orphan was taken by the nuns to their benevolent institution, where every attention was paid that humanity could suggest....

The river-side portion of the town is entirely mercantile. Its narrow, dirty streets and dark houses, with heavy iron shutters, have a disagreeable appearance, which cannot but make an unfavourable impression on the mind of a British traveller. The other portion of the town, however, is of a different character, and the houses are interspersed with gardens and pleasant walks, which looked very agreeable from the windows of the ballroom of the Nelson Hotel. This room, which is painted from top to bottom, the walls and ceiling, with a coarse imitation of groves and Canadian scenery, commands a superb view of the city, the river, and all the surrounding country, taking in the distant mountains of Chambly, the shores of the St Laurence, towards Laprairie, and the rapids above and below the island of St Anne's. The royal mountain (Mont Real), with its wooded sides, its rich scenery, and its city with its streets and public buildings, lie at your feet: with such objects before you the eye may well be charmed with the scenery of Montreal.

We receive the greatest attention from the master of the hotel, who is an Italian. The servants of the house are very civil, and the company that we meet are the ordinary very respectable, chiefly emigrants like ourselves, with some lively French men and women. The table is well supplied, and the charges for board and lodging one dollar per day each.

I am amused with the variety of characters of which our table is composed. Some of the emigrants appear to entertain the most sanguine hopes of success, appearing to foresee no difficulties in carrying their schemes into effect. As a contrast to these there is one of my countrymen, just returned from the western district on his way back to England, who entreats us by no means to go farther up this horrid country, as he emphatically styles the Upper Province, assuring us he would not live in it for all the land it contained.

He had been induced, by reading Cattermole's pamphlet on the subject of Emigration, to quit a good farm, and gathering together what property he possessed, to embark for Canada. Encouraged by the advice of a friend in this country, he purchased a lot of wild land in the western district; "but, sir," said he, addressing my husband with much vehemence, "I found I had been vilely deceived. Such land, such a country—I would not live in it for all I could see. Why, there is not a drop of wholesome water to be got, or a potato that is fit to eat. I lived for two months in a miserable shed they call a shanty, eaten up alive with mosquitoes. I could get nothing to eat but salted pork, and, in short, the discomforts are unbearable. And then all my farming knowledge was quite useless—people know nothing about farming in this country. Why, it would have broken my heart to work among the stumps, and never see such a thing as a well-ploughed field. And then," he added, in a softer tone, "I thought of my poor wife and the little one. I might, for the sake of bettering my condition, have roughed out a year or so myself, but, poor thing, I could not have had the heart to have brought her out from the comforts of England to such a place, not so good as one of our cow-houses or stables, and so I shall just go home; and if I don't tell all my neighbours what sort of a country this is they are all crazing to throw up their farms and come to, never trust a word of mine again."

It was to no purpose that some persons present argued with him on the folly of returning until he had tried what could be done: he only told them they were fools if they stayed an hour in a country like this; and ended by execrating those persons who deceived the people at home by their false statements, who sum up in a few pages all the advantages, without filling a volume with the disadvantages, as they might well do. . . .

Cobourg, August 29—When I closed my last letter I told you, my dear mother, that we should leave Montreal by sunrise the following day; but in this we were doomed to be disappointed, and to experience the truth of these words: "Boast not thyself of tomorrow, for thou knowest not what an hour may bring forth." Early that very morning, just an hour before sunrise, I was seized with the symptoms of the fatal malady that had made so many homes desolate. I was too ill to commence my journey, and, with a heavy heart, heard the lumbering wheels of the stage that we had taken our places in for Lachine rattle over the stones from the door of the hotel.

I hourly grew worse, till the sister of the landlady, an excellent young woman, who had previously shown me great attention, persuaded me to send for a physician; and my husband, distracted at seeing me in such agony, ran off to seek for the best medical aid. After some little delay a physician was found. I was then in extreme torture; but was relieved by bleeding, and by the violent fits of sickness that ensued. I will not dwell minutely on my sufferings; suffice to say, they were intense, but God, in His mercy, though He chastened and afflicted me, yet gave me not over unto death. From the females of the house I received the greatest kindness. Instead of fleeing affrighted from the chamber of sickness, the two Irish girls almost quarrelled which should be my attendant; while Jane Taylor, the good young woman I before mentioned, never left me from the time I grew so alarmingly ill till a change for the better had come over me, but, at the peril of her own life, supported me in her arms, and held me on her bosom when I was struggling with mortal agony, alternately speaking peace to me and striving to sooth the anguish of my poor afflicted partner.

The remedies applied were bleeding, a portion of opium, blue pill, and some sort of salts—not the common Epsom. The remedies proved effectual, though I suffered much from sickness and headache for many hours. The debility and low fever that took the place of the cholera, obliged me to keep my bed some days. During the first two my doctor visited me four times a day; he was very kind, and, on hearing that I was the wife of a British officer emigrating to the Upper Province, he seemed more than ever interested in my recovery, evincing a sympathy for us that was very grateful to our feelings. After a weary confinement of several days, I was at last pronounced in a sufficiently convalescent state to begin my journey, though still so weak that I was scarcely able to support myself. . . .

With the exception of Quebec and Montreal, I must give the preference to the Upper Province. If not on so grand a scale, the scenery is more calculated to please, from the appearance of industry and fertility it displays. I am delighted, in travelling along the road, with the neatness, cleanliness, and comfort of the cottages and farms. The log-house and shanty rarely occur, having been supplanted by pretty frame-houses, built in a superior style, and often painted white-lead colour or a pale pea-green. Around these habitations were orchards, bending down with a rich harvest of apples, plums, and the American crab, those beautiful little scarlet apples so often met with as a wet preserve among our sweetmeats at home.

You see none of the signs of poverty or its attendant miseries. No ragged, dirty, squalid children, dabbling in mud or dust; but many a tidy, smart-looking lass was spinning at the cottage-doors, with bright eyes and braided locks, while the younger girls were seated on the green turf or on the threshold, knitting and singing as blithe as birds.

There is something very picturesque in the great spinning-wheels that are used in this country for spinning wool, and if attitude were to be studied among our Canadian lasses, there cannot be one more becoming, or calculated to show off the natural advantages of a fine figure, than spinning at the big wheel. The spinster does not sit, but walks to and fro, guiding the yarn with one hand while with the other she turns the wheel.

I often noticed, as we passed by the cottage farms, hanks of yarn of different colours hanging on the garden or orchard fence to dry; there were all manner of colours, green, blue, purple, brown, red, and white. A civil landlady, at whose tavern we stopped to change horses, told me these hanks of yarn were first spun and then dyed by the good wives, preparatory to being sent to the loom. She showed me some of this home-spun cloth, which really looked very well. It was a dullish dark brown, the wool being the produce of a breed of black sheep. This cloth is made up in different ways for family use. A mixture of white and black wool gives the brown color, or else white dyed with Butternut.

"Every little dwelling you see," said she, "has its lot of land, and, consequently, its flock of sheep; and, as the children are early taught to spin and knit, and help to dye the yarn, their parents can afford to see them well and comfortably clothed.

"Many of these very farms you now see in so thriving a condition were wild land thirty years ago, nothing but Indian hunting-grounds. The industry of men, and many of them poor men, that had not a rood of land of their own in their own country, has effected this change."

I was much gratified by the reflection to which this good woman's information gave rise. "We also are going to purchase wild land, and why may not we see our farm, in process of time," thought I, "equal these fertile spots. Surely this is a blessed country to which we have emigrated," said I, pursuing the pleasing idea, "where every cottage abounds with the comforts and necessaries of life."

I perhaps overlooked at that time the labour, the difficulties, the privations to which these settlers had been exposed when they first came to this country. I saw it only at a distance of many years, under a high state of cultivation, perhaps in the hands of their children or their children's children, while the toil-worn parent's head was low in the dust.

Among other objects my attention was attracted by the appearance of open burying-grounds by the roadside. Pretty green mounds, surrounded by groups of walnut and other handsome timber trees, contained the graves of a family, or may be, some favoured friends slept quietly below the turf beside them. If the ground was not consecrated, it was hallowed by the tears and prayers of parents and children....

After some difficulty in obtaining sight of the landlady of the inn at Cornwall, and asking her to show me a chamber where we might pass the night, with a most ungracious air she pointed to a door which opened into a mere closet, in which was a bed divested of curtains, one chair, and an apology for a wash-stand. Seeing me in some dismay at the sight of this uninviting domicile, she laconically observed there was that or none, unless I chose to sleep in a four-bedded room, which had three tenants in it—and those gentlemen. This alternative I somewhat indignantly declined, and in no very good humour retired to my cabin, where vile familiars to the dormitory kept us from closing our weary eyelids till the break of day.

We took an early and hasty breakfast, and again commenced our journey. Here our party consisted of myself, my husband, a lady and gentleman with three small children, besides an infant of a month old, all of whom, from the eldest to the youngest, were suffering from whooping-cough; two great Cumberland miners, and a French pilot and his companion—this was a huge amphibious-looking monster, who bounced in and squeezed himself into a corner seat, giving a knowing nod and comical grin to the driver, who was in the secret, and who, in utter defiance of all remonstrance at this unlooked-for intrusion, cracked his whip with a flourish that appeared to be reckoned pretty considerably smart by two American travellers that stood on either side the door at the inn, with their hats not in their hands nor yet on their heads, but slung by a black ribbon to one of their waistcoat buttons, so as to fall nearly under one arm. This practice I have seen adopted since, and think if Johnny Gilpin had but taken this wise precaution he might have saved both hat and wig.

I was dreadfully fatigued with this day's travelling, being literally bruised black and blue. We suffered much inconvenience from the excessive heat of the day, and could well have dispensed with the company of two out of the four of our bulky companions.

We reached Prescott about five the same afternoon, where we met with good treatment at the inn; the female servants were all English, and seemed to vie with each other in attention to us. Here I was treated with a large tumbler of new milk by a Manx girl who was most kind to the English lads.

We saw little in the town of Prescott to interest or please. After an excellent breakfast we embarked on board the *Great Britain*, the finest steamer we had yet seen, and here we were joined by our new friends, to our great satisfaction.

At Brockville we arrived just in time to enjoy what was to me quite a novel sight—a ship-launch. A gay and exciting scene it was. The sun shone brilliantly on a concourse of people that thronged the shore in their holiday attire; the church bells rang merrily out, mingling with the music from the deck of this gaily painted vessel that, with flags and streamers, and a well-dressed company on board, was preparing for the launch.

To give additional effect, a salute was fired from a temporary fort erected for the occasion on a little rocky island in front of the town. The schooner took the water in fine style, as if eager to embrace the element which was henceforth to be subject to her. It was a moment of intense interest. The newly launched was greeted with three cheers from the company on board the *Great Britain*, with a salute from the little fort, and a merry peal from the bells, which were also rung in honour of a pretty bride that came on board with her bridegroom on their way to visit the falls of Niagara.

Brockville is just at the entrance of the Lake of the Thousand Islands, and presents a pretty appearance from the water. The town has improved rapidly, I am told, within the last few years, and is becoming a place of some importance.

The shores of the St Laurence assume a more rocky and picturesque aspect as you advance among its thousand islands, which present every variety of wood and rock. The steamer put in for a supply of fire-wood at a little village on the American side the river, where also we took on board five-and-twenty beautiful horses, which are to be exhibited at Cobourg and York (Toronto) for sale.

There was nothing at all worthy of observation in the American village, unless I except a novelty that rather amused me. Almost every house had a tiny wooden model of itself, about the bigness of a doll's house, stuck up in front of the roof or at the gable end. I was informed by a gentleman on board these baby-houses were for the swallows to build in.

It was midnight when we passed Kingston, so of course I saw nothing of that "key to the lakes." When I awoke in the morning the steamer was dashing gallantly along through the waters of the Ontario, and I experienced a slight sensation of sickness.

When the waters of the lake are at all agitated, as they sometimes are, by high winds, you might imagine yourself upon a tempest-tossed sea.

The shores of the Ontario are very fine, rising in waving lines of hill and dale, clothed with magnificent woods, or enlivened by patches of cultivated land and pretty dwellings. At ten o'clock we reached Cobourg.

Cobourg, at which place we are at present, is a neatly built and flourishing village, containing many good stores, mills, a banking-house, and printing-office, where a newspaper is published once a week. There is a very pretty church and a select society, many families of respectability having fixed their residences in or near the town....

CHAPTER 5 *First Problems of Backwoods*

Peterborough, Newcastle District,
September 9, 1832.

We left Cobourg on the afternoon of the 1st of September in a light waggon, comfortably lined with buffalo robes. Our fellow-travellers consisted of three gentlemen and a young lady, all of whom proved very agreeable, and willing to afford us every information respecting the country through which we were travelling. The afternoon was fine—one of those rich mellow days we often experience in the early part of September. The warm hues of autumn were already visible on the forest trees, but spoke rather of ripeness than decay. The country around Cobourg is well cultivated, a great portion of the woods having been superseded by open fields, pleasant farms, and fine flourishing orchards, with green pastures, where abundance of cattle were grazing.

The country gaol and court-house at Amherst, about a mile and a half from Cobourg, is a fine stone edifice, situated on a rising ground which commands an extensive view over the lake Ontario and surrounding scenery. As you advance farther up the country northward, in the direction of Hamilton or Rice Lake plains, the land rises into bold sweeping hills and dales, and again descends to the valley of the Rice Lake. Beyond this beautiful lake the land again rises in graceful sweeps northward.

The outline of the country reminded me of the hilly part of Gloucestershire; you want, however, the charm with which civilization has so eminently adorned that fine county, with all its romantic villages, flourishing towns, cultivated farms, and extensive downs, so thickly covered with flocks and herds. Here the bold forests of oak, beech, maple, and basswood, with now and then a grove of dark pine, cover the hills, only enlivened by an occasional settlement, with its log-house and zig-zag fences of split timber: these fences are very offensive to my eye. I look in vain for the rich hedgerows of my native country. Even the stone fences in the north and west of England, cold and bare as they are, are less unsightly. The settlers, however, invariably adopt whatever plan saves time, labour and money. The great law of expediency is strictly observed; it is born of necessity. Matters of taste appear to be little regarded, or are, at all events, after-considerations. Very few specimens of the old log-house and shanty can be seen, but many good farm-houses and neat fences.

I could see a smile hover on the lips of my fellow-travellers on hearing of our projected plans for the adornment of our future dwelling.

"If you go into the backwoods your house must necessarily be a log-house," said an elderly gentleman, who had been a settler many years in the country, "for you will most probably be out of the way of a saw-mill, and you will find so much to do, and so many obstacles to encounter, for the first two or three years, that you will hardly have opportunity for carrying these improvements into effect."

"There is an old saying," he added, with a mixture of gravity and good humour in his looks, "that I used to hear when I was a boy, 'first creep and then go.' Matters are not carried on quite so easily here as at home; and the truth of this a very few weeks' acquaintance with the bush, as we term all unbroken forest land, will prove. At the end of ten or fifteen years you may begin to talk of these pretty improvements and elegancies, and you will then be able to see a little what you are about. . . ."

We now ascended the plains—a fine elevation of land—for many miles scantily clothed with oaks, and here and there bushy pines, with other trees and shrubs. The soil is in some places sandy, but varies, I am told, considerably in different parts, and is covered in large tracts with rich herbage, affording abundance of the finest pasture for cattle. A number of exquisite flowers and shrubs adorn these plains, which rival any garden in beauty during the spring and summer months. Many of these plants are peculiar to the plains, and are rarely met with in any other situation. The trees, too, though inferior in size to those in the forests, are more picturesque, growing in groups or singly, at considerable intervals, giving a sort of park-like appearance to this portion of the country. The prevailing opinion seems to be, that the plains, laid out in grazing or dairy farms, would answer the purpose of settlers well as there is plenty of land that will grow wheat and other corn-crops, and can be improved at a small expense, besides abundance of natural pasture for cattle. One great advantage seems to be that the plough can be introduced directly, and the labour of preparing the ground is necessarily much less than where it is wholly covered with wood. The soil is chiefly a fine yellow loam on a clayey subsoil and produces the best of wheat and other grain, roots and vegetables of every kind, but the process of clearing the land is one of much labour.

There are several settlers on these plains possessing considerable farms. The situation, I should think, must be healthy and agreeable, from the elevation and dryness of the land, and the pleasant prospect they command of the country below them, especially where the Rice Lake, with its various islands and picturesque shores is visible. The ground itself is pleasingly broken into hill and valley, sometimes gently sloping, at other times abrupt and almost precipitous.

An American farmer, who formed one of our party at breakfast the following morning, told me that these plains were formerly famous hunting-grounds of the Indians, who, to prevent the growth of the timbers, burned them year after year, this, in process of time destroying the young trees, so as to prevent them again from accumulating to the extent they formerly did. Sufficient only was left to form coverts; for the deer resort hither in great herds for the sake of a peculiar tall sort of grass with which these plains abound, called deer-grass, on which they became exceedingly fat at certain seasons of the year.

Evening closed in before we reached the tavern on the shores of the Rice Lake, where we were to pass the night; so that I lost something of the beautiful scenery which this fine expanse of water presents as you descend the plains towards its shores. The glimpses I caught of it were by the faint but frequent flashes of lightning that illumined the horizon to the north, which just revealed enough to make me regret I could see no more that night. The Rice Lake is prettily diversified with small wooded islets: the north bank rises gently from the water's edge. Within sight of Sully the tavern from which the steamboat starts that goes up the Otonabee, you see several well-cultivated settlements; and beyond the Indian village the missionaries have a school for the education and instruction of the Indian children. Many of them can both read and write fluently, and are greatly improved in their moral and religious conduct. They are well and comfortably clothed, and have houses to live in. But they are still too much attached to their wandering habits to become good and industrious settlers. During certain seasons they leave the village and encamp themselves in the woods along the borders of those lakes and rivers that present the most advantageous hunting and fishing-grounds.

The Rice Lake and Mud Lake Indians belong, I am told, to the Chippewas; but the traits of cunning and warlike ferocity that formerly marked this singular people seem to have disappeared beneath the milder influence of Christianity. . . .

As I felt a great curiosity to see the interior of a log-house, I entered the open door-way of the tavern, as the people termed it, under the pretext of buying a draught of milk. The interior of this rude dwelling presented no very inviting aspect. The walls were of rough, unhewn logs, filled between the chinks with moss and irregular wedges of wood to keep out the wind and rain. The unplastered roof displayed the rafters, covered with moss and lichens, green, yellow, and grey; above which might be seen the shingles, dyed to a fine mahogany-red by the smoke which refused to ascend the wide clay and stone chimney, to curl gracefully about the roof, and seeks its exit in the various crannies and apertures with which the roof and sides of the building abounded.

The floor was of earth, which had become pretty hard and smooth through use. This hut reminded me of the one described by the four Russian sailors that were left to winter on the island of Spitzbergen. Its furniture was of corresponding rudeness: a few stools, rough and unplaned; a deal table, which, from being manufactured from unseasoned wood, was divided by three wide-open seams, and was only held together by its ill-shaped legs; two or three blocks of grey limestone placed beside the hearth served for seats for the children, with the addition of two beds raised a little above the ground by a frame of split cedars. On these lowly couches lay extended two poor men, suffering under the wasting effects of lake-fever. Their yellow bilious faces strangely contrasted with the gay patchwork-quilts that covered them. I felt much concerned for the poor emigrants, who told me they had not been many weeks in the country when they were seized with the fever and ague. They both had wives and small children, who seemed very miserable. The wives also had been sick with ague, and had not a house or even shanty of their own up; the husbands having fallen ill were unable to earn anything; and much of the little money they had brought out with them had been expended in board and lodging in this miserable place, which they dignified by the name of a tavern. I cannot say I was greatly prepossessed in favour of their hostess, a harsh, rude woman. Besides the various emigrants, men, women, and children, that lodged within the walls, the log-house had tenants of another description. A fine calf occupied a pen in a corner; some pigs roamed grunting about in company with some half-dozen fowls. The most attractive objects were three snow-white pigeons that were meekly picking up crumbs, and looking as if they were too pure and innocent to be inhabitants of such a place.

Owing to the shallowness of the river at this season, and to the rapids, the steamboat is unable to go up the whole way to Peterborough, and a scow or rowboat, as it is sometimes termed —a huge, unwieldly, flat-bottomed machine—meets the passengers at a certain part of the river, within sight of a singular pine-tree on the right bank; this is termed the "Yankee bonnet," from the fancied resemblance of the topmost boughs to a sort of cap worn by the Yankees, not much unlike the blue bonnet of Scotland. Some call this tree "Scotch bonnet."

Unfortunately, the steamer ran aground some four miles below the usual place of rendezvous, and we waited till near four o'clock for the scow. When it made its appearance, we found, to our discomfort, the rowers (eight in number, and all Irishmen) were under the exciting influence of whiskey, which they had drunk on the voyage. They were, moreover, exasperated by the delay on the part of the steamer, which gave them four miles additional heavy rowing. Besides a number of passengers there was an enormous load of furniture, trunks, boxes, chests, sacks of wheat, barrels of flour, salt, and pork, with many miscellaneous packages and articles, small and great, which were piled to a height that I thought very unsafe both to goods and passengers.

With a marvellous ill-grace the men took up their oars when

their load was completed, but declared they would go on shore and make a fire and cook their dinners, they not having eaten any food, though they had taken large potations of the whiskey. This measure was opposed by some of the gentlemen, and a fierce and angry scene ensued, which ended in the mutineers flinging down their oars and positively refusing to row another stroke till they had satisfied their hunger.

Perhaps I had a fellow-feeling for them, as I began to be exceedingly hungry, almost ravenous, myself. I had tasted no food that morning before starting, and previous illness had weakened me. Indeed, so faint was I that I was fain to get my husband to procure me a morsel of the coarse, uninviting bread that was produced by the rowers, and which they ate with huge slices of uncooked pickled pork, seasoning this unseemly meal with curses "not loud, but deep," and bitter taunts against those who prevented them from eating their food like *Christians*.

While I was eagerly looking at the bit of bread, an old farmer, who had eyed me for some time with a mixture of curiosity and compassion, said, "Poor thing! Well, you do seem hungry indeed, and I dare say are just out from the *ould* country, and so little used to such hard fare. Here are some cakes that my woman (*i.e.*, wife) put in my pocket when I left home; I care nothing for them, but they are better than that bad bread; take 'em, and welcome." With these words he tossed some very respectable home-made seed-cakes into my lap, and truly never was anything more welcome than this seasonable refreshment.

A sullen and gloomy spirit seemed to prevail among our boatmen, which by no means diminished as the evening drew on and "the rapids were near." The sun had set, and the moon and stars rose brilliantly over the still waters, which gave back the reflection of this glorious multitude of heavenly bodies. A sight so passing fair might have stilled the most turbulent spirits into peace; at least so I thought, as, wrapped in my cloak, I leant back against he supporting arm of my husband, looking from the waters to the sky, and from the sky to the waters. My pleasant reverie was, however, soon ended, when I suddenly felt the boat touch the rocky bank, and heard the boatmen protesting they would go no farther that night. We were nearly two miles below Peterborough, and how I was to walk this distance, weakened as I was by recent illness and the fatigue of our long travelling, I knew not. To spend the night in an open boat, exposed to the heavy dews arising from the river, would be almost death. While we were deliberating on what to do, the rest of the passengers had made up their minds, and taken the way through the woods by a road they were well acquainted with. They were soon out of sight, all but one gentleman, who was bargaining with one of the rowers to take him and his dog across the river at the head of the rapids in a skiff.

Imagine our situation, at ten o'clock at night, without knowing a single step of our road, put on shore to find the way to the distant town as we best could, or pass the night in the dark forest.

Almost in despair, we entreated the gentleman to be our guide as far as he went. But so many obstacles beset our path in the form of newly chopped trees and blocks of stone, scattered along the shore, that it was with the utmost difficulty we could keep him in sight. At last we came up with him at the place appointed to meet the skiff, and, with a pertinacity that at another time and in other circumstances we never should have adopted, my husband bought a passage in the skiff as I was unable to walk any farther. An angry, growling consent was extorted from the surly Charon, and we hastily entered the frail bark, which seemed hardly calculated to convey us in safety to the opposite shore. I could not help indulging in a feeling of indescribable fear as I listened to the torrent of profane invective that burst forth continually from the lips of the boatman. Once or twice we were in danger of being overset by the boughs of the pines and cedars which had fallen into the water near the banks. Right glad was I when we reached the opposite shores; but here a new trouble arose: there was yet more untracked wood to cross before we again met the skiff which had to pass up a small rapid, and meet us at the head of "Little Lake," an expansion of the Otonabee a little below Peterborough. At the distance of every few yards our path was obstructed by fallen trees, mostly hemlock, spruce, or cedar, the branches of which are so thickly interwoven that it is scarcely possible to separate them, or force a passage through the tangled thicket which they form.

Had it not been for the humane assistance of our conductor, I know not how I should have surmounted these difficulties. Sometimes I was ready to sink down from very weariness. At length I hailed, with a joy I could hardly have supposed possible, the gruff voice of the Irish rower, and, after considerable grumbling on his part, we were again seated.

Glad enough we were to see, by the blazing light of an enormous log-heap, the house of our new friend. But the lady of the house refused us shelter for the night, and her lord and master sent a little Irish boy to guide us to the town. His frankness and good humour quite won our regards. He informed us he was one of seven orphans, who had lost father and mother in the cholera. It was a sad thing, he said, to be left fatherless and motherless, in a strange land; and he swept away the tears that gathered in his eyes as he told the simple, but sad tale of his early bereavement; but added, cheerfully, he had met with a kind master, who had taken some of his brothers and sisters into his service as well as himself.

Just as we were emerging from the gloom of the wood we found our progress impeded by a *creek*, as the boy called it, over which he told us we must pass by a log-bridge before we could get to the town. Now, the log bridge was composed of one log, or rather a fallen tree, thrown across the stream, rendered very slippery by the heavy dew that had risen from the swamp. As the long admitted of only one person at a time, I could receive no assistance from my companions; and, though our little guide, with a natural politeness arising from the benevolence of his disposition, did me all the service in his power by holding the lantern close to the surface to throw all the light he could on the subject, I had the ill luck to fall in up to my knees in the water, my head turning quite giddy as I came to the last step or two; thus was I wet as well as weary. To add to our misfortune we saw the lights disappear, one by one, in the village, till a solitary candle, glimmering from the upper chambers of one or two houses, were our only beacons. We had yet a lodging to seek, and it was near midnight before we reached the door of the only inn. Here, at least, thought I, our troubles for tonight will end; but great was our mortification on being told there was not a spare bed to be had in the house, every one being occupied by emigrants going up to one of the back townships.

Our good hostess insisted on giving up her own sleeping-room and bed for us, and taking heed of my weary looks introduced us into our dormitory. What would my English friends have said could they have seen the room in which my first night in Peterborough was passed? Truly it looked like a bird-cage rather than a bed-chamber. The walls were of lath, unplastered and open so that the cool night breeze blew freshly through the bars and I could see the white frothy water of the rapids of the river dancing in the moonlight as I lay in my bed, and hear the musical ripple as it rushed past the bank on which the house was built. It was a new experience and wonderful to say, I slept soundly and took no cold from the air bath or bath in the creek, but did not waken until the sun had long risen in the clear blue, cloudless sky and the inmates of the house were all astir....

CHAPTER 6 *Peterborough and Environs*

Peterborough, Sept. 11, 1832.

Here follows the original part of my Journal, from leaving my rest in Peterborough to the arrival in upper Douro.

It is now settled that we abide here till after the Government sale has taken place. We are then to remain with my brother S—— in his family till we have got a few acres chopped and a log-house put up on our own land. Having determined to go at once into the bush, on account of our military grant, which we have been so fortunate as to draw in the neighbourhood of S——, we have fully made up our minds to enter at once, and cheerfully, on the privations and inconveniences attending such a situation; as there is no choice between relinquishing that great advantage and doing our settlement duties. We shall not be worse off than others who have gone before us to the unsettled townships, many of whom, naval and military officers, with their families, have had to struggle with considerable difficulties, but who are now beginning to feel the advantages arising from their exertions.

In addition to the land he is entiled to as an officer in the British service, my husband is in treaty for the purchase of an eligible lot higher up the lake. A creek divides our lot from my brother's settlement. This will give us a water frontage, and a further inducement to bring us within a little distance of S——;

so that we shall not be quite so lonely as if we had gone on to our Government lot at once, which would have taken us into a lonely, uncleared wilderness far from any settlement. . . .

But it is now time I should give you some account of Peterborough, which, in point of situation, is superior to any place I have yet seen in the Upper Province. It occupies a central point between the townships of Monaghan, Smith, Cavan, Otonabee, and Douro, and may with propriety be considered as the capital of the district.

It is situated on a fine elevated plain, just above the small lake, where the river is divided by two low wooded islets. The original or Government part of the town is laid out in half-acre lots; the streets, which are now fast filling up, are nearly at right angles with the river, and extend towards the plains to the northeast. These plains form a beautiful natural park, finely diversified with hill and dale, covered with a lovely green sward, enamelled with a variety of the most exquisite flowers, and planted, as if by Nature's own hand, with groups of feathery pines, oaks, balsams, poplars, and silver birches. The views from these plains are delightful; whichever way you turn your eyes they are gratified by a diversity of hill and dale, wood and water, with the town spreading over a considerable tract of ground.

The plains descend with a steep declivity towards the river, which rushes with considerable impetuosity between its banks. Fancy a long, narrow valley separating the east and west portions of the town into two distinct villages.

The Otonabee bank rises to a loftier elevation than the Monaghan side, and commands an extensive view over the intervening valley, the opposite town, and the boundary forest and hills behind it: this is called Peterborough East, and is in the hands of two or three individuals of large capital, from whom the town lots are purchased.

Peterborough thus divided covers a great extent of ground, more than sufficient for the formation of a large city. The number of inhabitants is now reckoned at seven hundred and upwards, and if it continues to increase as rapidly in the next few years as it has done lately it will soon be a very populous town.

There is great water-power, both as regards the river and the fine broad creek which winds its way through the town and falls into the small lake below. There are several saw- and grist-mills, a distillery, fulling-mill, two principal inns, besides smaller ones, a number of good stores, a Government school-house, which also serves for a church till one more suitable should be built. The plains are sold off in park lots, and some pretty little dwellings are being built, but I much fear the natural beauties of this lovely spot will be soon spoiled.

I am never weary with strolling about, climbing the hills in every direction, to catch some new prospect or gather some new flowers, which, though getting late in the summer, are still abundant.

Among the plants with whose names I am acquainted are a variety of shrubby asters, of every tint of blue, purple, and pearly white; a lilac *monarda*, most delightfully aromatic, even to the dry stalks and seed-vessels; the white *gnaphalium* or everlasting flower; roses of several kinds, a few late buds of which I found in a valley near the church. I also noticed among the shrubs a very pretty little plant resembling our box; it trails along the ground, sending up branches and shoots; the leaves turn of a deep copper red;* yet, in spite of this contradiction, it is an evergreen. I also noticed some beautiful lichens,† with coral caps surmounting the grey hollow foot-stalks, which grow in irregular tufts among the dry mosses, or more frequently I found them covering the roots of the trees or half-decayed timbers. Among a variety of fungi I gathered a hollow cup of the most splendid scarlet within and a pale fawn colour without. Another very beautiful fungus consisted of small branches like clusters of white coral, but of so delicate a texture that the slightest touch caused them to break.

The ground in many places was covered with a thick carpet of strawberries of many varieties, which afford a constant dessert during the season to those who choose to pick them, a privilege of which I am sure I should gladly avail myself were I near them in the summer. Beside the plants I have myself observed in blossom, I am told the spring and summer produce many others: the orange lily (*Lilium Philadelphicum*); the phlox, or purple *lichnidea*; the moccasin flower, or ladies' slipper (*Cyprepedium pubescens*); lilies of the valley (*Canadensis bifolia*) in abundance and, towards the banks of the creek and the Otonabee, the splendid cardinal flower (*lobelia cardinalis*) waves its scarlet spikes of blossoms. . . .

* *Uva-ursi*. Bear-berry. † Claytonia.

On Sunday I went to church, the first opportunity I had had of attending public worship since I was in the Highlands of Scotland; and surely I had reason to bow my knees in thankfulness to that merciful God who had brought us through the perils of the great deep and the horrors of the pestilence.

Never did our beautiful liturgy seem so touching and impressive as it did that day, offered up in our lowly log-built church in the wilderness.

This simple edifice is situated at the foot of a gentle slope on the plains, surrounded by groups of oak and feathery pines, which, though inferior in point of size to the huge pines and oaks of the forest, are far more agreeable to the eye, branching out in a variety of fantastic forms. The turf here is of an emerald greenness: in short, it is a sweet spot, retired from the noise and bustle of the town, a fitting place in which to worship God in spirit and in truth....

The shanty is a sort of primitive hut in Canadian architecture, and is nothing more than a shed built of logs, the chinks between the round edges of the timbers being filled with mud, moss, and bits of wood; the roof is frequently composed of logs split and hollowed with the axe, and placed side by side, so that the edges rest on each other; the concave and convex surfaces being alternately uppermost, every other log forms a channel to carry off the rain and melting snow. The eaves of this building resemble the scalloped edges of a clam shell; but, rude as this covering is, it effectually answers the purpose of keeping the interior dry; far more so than the roofs formed of bark or boards, through which the rain will find entrance. Sometimes the shanty has a window, sometimes only an open doorway, which admits the light and lets out the smoke. A rude chimney, which is often nothing better than an opening cut in one of the top logs above the hearth, a few boards fastened in a square form, serves as the vent for the smoke; the only precaution against the fire catching the log walls behind the hearth being a few large stones placed in a half circular form, or more commonly a bank of clay raised against the wall.

Nothing can be more comfortless than some of these shanties, reeking with smoke and dirt, the common receptacle for children, pigs, and fowls. But I have given you the dark side of the picture; I am happy to say all the shanties on the squatters' ground were not like these: on the contrary, by far the larger proportion were inhabited by tidy folks, and had one, or even two small windows, and a clay chimney regularly built up through the roof; some were even roughly floored, and possessed similar comforts with the small log-houses. . . .

I have already seen two of our poor neighbours that left the parish a twelvemonth ago; they are settled on Canada Company lots, and are getting on well. They have some few acres cleared and cropped, but are obliged to *hire out* to enable their families to live, working on their own land when they can. The men are in good spirits, and say they "shall in a few years have many comforts about them that they never could have got at home had they worked late and early; but they complain that their wives are always pining for home, and lamenting that ever they crossed the seas." This seems to be the general complaint with all classes; the women are discontented and unhappy. Few enter with their whole heart into a settler's life. They miss the little domestic comforts they had been used to enjoy; they regret the friends and relations they left in the old country; and they cannot endure the loneliness of the backwoods.

This prospect does not discourage me: I know I shall plenty of occupation within-doors, and I have sources of enjoyment when I walk abroad that will keep me from being dull. Besides, have I not a right to be cheerful and contented for the sake of my beloved partner? The change is not greater for me than for him; and if for his sake I have voluntarily left home, and friends, and country, shall I therefore sadden him by useless regrets? I am always inclined to subscribe to that sentiment of my favourite poet, Goldsmith,—

> Still to ourselves in every place consign'd,
> Our own felicity we make or find.

But I shall very soon be put to the test, as we leave this town tomorrow by ten o'clock. The purchase of the Lake lot is concluded. There are three acres chopped and a shanty up; but the shanty is not a habitable dwelling, being merely an open shed that was put up by the choppers as a temporary shelter; so we shall have to build a house. Late enough we are; too late to get in a full crop, as the land is merely chopped, not cleared, and it is too late now to log and burn the fallow and get the seed-wheat in: but it will be ready for spring crops. We paid five dollars and a half per acre for the lot; this was rather high for wild land so far from a town and in a scantily settled part of the township; but the situation is good, and has a water frontage, for which my husband was willing to pay something more than if the lot had been further inland.

In all probability it will be some time before I find leisure again to take up my pen. We shall remain guests with S—— till our house is in a habitable condition, which I suppose will be about Christmas.

CHAPTER 7 *Journey Through the Woods*

October 25, 1832.

. . . After some difficulty we succeeded in hiring a wagon and span (*i.e.* pair abreast) of stout horses to convey us and our luggage through the woods to the banks of one of the lakes, where S—— had appointed to ferry us across. There was no palpable road, only a blaze on the other side, the Douro side, encumbered by fallen trees, and interrupted by cedar swamps, into which one might sink up to one's knees, unless we took the precaution to step along the trunks of the mossy, decaying logs, or make our footing sure on some friendly block of granite or limestone. What is termed in bush language a *blaze*, is nothing more than notches or slices cut off the bark of the trees to mark out the line of road. The boundaries of the different lots are often marked by a blazed tree, also the concession-lines. These blazes are of as much use as finger-posts of a dark night.

The road we were compelled to take lay over the Peterborough plains, in the direction of the river; the scenery of which pleased me much, though it presents little appearance of fertility, with the exception of two or three extensive clearings.

About three miles above Peterborough the road winds along the brow of a steep ridge, the bottom of which has every appearance of having been formerly the bed of the present river, perhaps some small lake, which has been diverted from its channel and merged in the Otonabee.

On either side of this ridge there is a steep descent; on the right the Otonabee breaks upon you, rushing with great velocity over its rocky bed, forming rapids in miniature resembling those of the St Laurence; its dark, frowning woods of sombre pine, oak and maple, give a grandeur to the scenery that is very impressive. On the left lies below you a sweet secluded dell of evergreens, cedar, hemlock, and pine, enlivened by a few deciduous trees. Through this dell there is a roadtrack leading to a fine cleared farm, the green pastures of which were rendered more pleasing by the absence of the odious stumps that disfigure the clearings in this part of the country. A pretty, bright stream flows through the low meadow that lies at the foot of the hill, which you descend suddenly close by a small grist-mill that is worked by the waters, just where they meet the rapids of the river.

I called this place "Glen Morrison," partly from the remembrance of the lovely Glen Morrison of the Highlands, and partly because it was the name of the settler that owned the spot.

Our progress was but slow on account of the roughness of the road, which is beset with innumerable obstacles in the shape of loose blocks of limestone, with which the lands on the banks of the river and lakes abound; to say nothing of fallen trees, big roots, mud-holes, and corduroy bridges over which you go jolt, jolt, jolt, till every bone in your body feels as if it were being dislocated. An experienced bush-traveller avoids many hard thumps by rising up or clinging to the sides of his rough vehicle.

As the day was particularly fine, I often quitted the waggon and walked on with my husband for a mile or so.

We soon lost sight entirely of the river, and struck into the deep solitude of the forest, where not a sound disturbed the almost awful stillness that reigned around us. Scarcely a leaf or bough was in motion, excepting at intervals we caught the sound of the breeze stirring the lofty heads of the pine-trees, and wakening a hoarse and mournful cadence.

There was no passable road on the Douro side. I had to cross the river at Auburn—to the south side—and to re-cross to Douro again at the narrows to get to my brother's house, rather a round-about route. The tapping of the red-headed woodpeckers on the trunks of the decaying trees, and the shrill whistling cry of the little striped squirrel, called by the natives "chitmunk," were the only sounds that broke the stillness of the wild. I was surprised at the absence of animal life. With the exception of the aforesaid chitmunk, no living thing crossed our path during our long day's journey in the woods.

I was disappointed in the forest trees, having pictured to myself hoary giants almost primeval with the country itself, as greatly exceeding in majesty of form the trees of my native isles as the vast lakes and mighty rivers of Canada exceed the lakes and streams of Britain.

There is a want of picturesque beauty in the woods. The young growth of timber alone has any pretension to elegance of form, unless I except the hemlocks, which are extremely light and graceful, and of a lovely refreshing tint of green. Even when winter has stripped the forest it is still beautiful and verdant. The young beeches, too, are pretty enough, but you miss that fantastic bowery shade that is so delightful in our parks and woodlands at home.

There is no appearance of venerable antiquity in the Canadian woods. There are no ancient spreading oaks that might be called the patriarchs of the forest. A premature decay seems to be their doom. They are uprooted by the storm, and sink as they grow aged, to give place to a new generation that is ready to fill their places.

The pines are certainly the finest trees. In point of size there are none to surpass them. They tower above all the others, forming a dark line that may be distinguished for many miles. The pines, being so much loftier than the other trees, are sooner uprooted, as they receive the full and unbroken force of the wind in their tops; thus it is that the ground is continually strewn with the decaying trunks of huge pines. They also seem more liable to inward decay, and blasting from lightning, and insects. Dead pines are more frequently met with than any other tree.

Much as I had seen and heard of the badness of the roads in Canada, I was not prepared for such a one as we travelled along this day: indeed, it hardly deserved the name of a road, being little more than an opening hewed out through the woods, the trees being felled and drawn aside so as to admit a wheeled carriage passing along.

The swamps and little forest streams, that occasionally gush across the path, are rendered passable by logs placed side by side. From the ridgy and striped appearance of these bridges they are aptly enough termed corduroy.

Over these abominable corduroys the vehicle jolts, jumping from log to log, with a shock that must be endured with as good grace as possible. If you could bear these knocks, and pitiless thumpings and bumpings, without wry faces, your patience and philosophy would far exceed mine; sometimes I laughed because I would not cry.

Imagine me perched up on a seat composed of carpet-bags, trunks, and sundry packages, in a vehicle little better than a great rough deal box set on wheels, the sides being merely pegged in so that more than once I found myself in rather an awkward predicament, owing to the said sides falling out. In the very midst of a deep mud-hole out went the front board, and with the shock went the teamster (driver), who looked rather confounded at finding himself lodged just in the middle of a slough, reminding one of the "Slough of Despond." For my part, as I could do no good, I kept my seat, and patiently awaited the restoration to order. This was soon effected, and all went on well again till a jolt against a huge pine-tree gave such a jar to the ill-set vehicle that one of the boards danced out that composed the bottom, and a sack of flour and a bag of salted pork, which were on the way to a settler's, whose clearing we had to pass in the way, were ejected. A good teamster is seldom taken aback by such trifles as these. He is, or should be, provided with an axe. No waggon, team, or any other travelling equipage should be unprovided with an instrument of this kind, as no one can answer for the obstacles that may impede his progress in the bush. The disasters we met fortunately required but little skill in remedying. The sides need only a stout peg, and the loosened planks that form the bottom being quickly replaced, away we went again over root, stump, and stone, mud-hole, and corduroy; now against the trunk of some standing tree, now mounting over some fallen one, with an impulse that would annihilate any lighter equipage than a Canadian waggon, which is admirably fitted by its very roughness for such roads as we have in the bush.

The sagacity of the horses of this country is truly admirable. Their patience in surmounting the difficulties they have to encounter, their skill in avoiding the holes and stones, and in making their footing sure over the round and slippery timbers of the log-bridges, render them very valuable. If they want the spirit and fleetness of some of our high-bred blood-horses, they make up in gentleness, strength, and patience. This renders them most truly valuable, as they will travel in such places that no British horse would, with equal safety to their drivers. Nor are the Canadian horses, when well fed and groomed, at all deficient in beauty of color, size, or form. They are not very often used in logging; the ox is preferred in all rough and heavy labour of this kind on wild land.

Just as the increasing gloom of the forest began to warn us of the approach of evening, and I was getting weary and hungry, our driver, in some confusion, avowed his belief that, somehow or other, he had missed the track, though how he could not tell, seeing there was but one road. We were nearly two miles from the last settlement, and he said we ought to be within sight of the lake if we were on the right track. The only plan, we agreed, was for him to go forward and leave the team, and endeavour to ascertain if he were near the water, and if otherwise, to return to the house we had passed and inquire the way.

After running full half a mile ahead he returned with a dejected countenance, saying we must be wrong, for he saw no appearance of water, and the road we were on appeared to end in a cedar swamp, as the farther he went the thicker the hemlocks and cedars became; so, as we had no desire to commence our settlement by a night's lodging in a dismal swamp—where, to use the expression of our driver, the cedars grew as thick as hairs on a cat's back—we agreed to retrace our steps.

After some difficulty the lumbering machine was turned, and slowly we began our backward march. We had not gone more than a mile when a boy came along, who told us we might just go back again, as there was no other road to the lake; and added, with a knowing nod of his head, "Master, I guess if you had known the bush as well as I you would never have been *fule* enough to turn when you were going just right. Why, anybody knows that *them* cedars and himlocks grow thickest near the water; so you may just go back for your pains."

It was dark, save that the stars came forth with more than usual brilliancy, when we suddenly emerged from the depth of the gloomy forest to the shores of a beautiful lake that gleamed the more brightly from the contrast of the dark masses of foliage that hung over it, and the towering pinewoods that girt its banks.

Here, seated on a huge block of limestone, which was covered with a soft cushion of moss, beneath the shade of the cedars that skirt the lake, surrounded with trunks, boxes and packages of various descriptions, which the driver had hastily thrown from the waggon, I sat in anxious expectation of some answering voice to my husband's long and repeated halloo to rouse my brother and his men.

But when the echo of his voice had died away we heard only the gurgling of the waters at the head of the rapids, and the distant and hoarse murmur of a waterfall some half mile below them.

We could see no sign of any habitation, no gleam of light from the shore to cheer us. In vain we strained our ears for the plash of the oar, or welcome sound of the human voice, or bark of some household dog, that might assure us we were not doomed to pass the night in the lone wood.

We began now to apprehend we had really lost the way. To attempt returning through the deepening darkness of the forest in search of anyone to guide us was quite out of the question, the road being so ill defined that we should soon have been lost in the mazes of the woods. The last sound of the waggon-wheels had died away in the distance; to have overtaken it would have been impossible. Bidding me remain quietly where I was, my husband forced his way through the tangled underwood along the bank, in the hope of discovering some sign of the house we sought, which we had every reason to suppose must be near, though probably hidden by the dense mass of trees from our sight....

At last my reverie was broken by the light plash of a paddle, and a bright line of light showed a canoe dancing over the lake: in a few minutes a well-known and friendly voice greeted me as the little bark was moored among the cedars at my feet. My husband having gained a projecting angle of the shore, had discovered the welcome blaze of the wood fire in the log-house, and, after some difficulty had succeeded by his loud halloo in rousing the attention of its inhabitants. Our coming that day had long been given up, and our first call had been mistaken for the sound of ox-bells in the wood: this had caused the delay that had so embarrassed us.

We soon forgot our weary wanderings beside the bright fire that blazed on the hearth of the log-house, in which we found S—— comfortably domiciled with his wife. To my sister-in-law

I was duly introduced; and, in spite of all the remonstrances from the affectionate and careful mother, three fair sleeping children were successively handed out of their cribs to be shown me by the proud and delighted father.

Our welcome was given with that unaffected cordiality that is so grateful to the heart: it was as sincere as it was kind. All means were adopted to soften the roughness of our accommodation, which, if it lacked that elegance and convenience to which we had been accustomed in England, was not devoid of rustic comfort; at all events it was such as many settlers of the first respectability have been glad to content themselves with, and many have not been half so well lodged as we now are.

We may indeed consider ourselves fortunate in not being obliged to go at once into the rude shanty that I described to you as the only habitation on our land. This test of our fortitude was kindly spared us by S——, who insisted on our remaining beneath his hospitable roof till such time as we should have put up a house on our own lot. Here then we are for the present *fixed*, as the Canadians say; and if I miss many of the little comforts and luxuries of life, I enjoy excellent health and spirits, and am very happy in the society of those around me, so faithful and true.

The children are already very fond of me. They have discovered my passion for flowers, which they diligently search for among the stumps and along the lake shore. I have begun collecting, and though the season is far advanced, my *hortus siccus* boasts of several elegant specimens of fern; the yellow Canadian violet, which blooms twice in the year, in the spring and fall, as the autumnal season is expressively termed; two sorts of Michaelmas daisies, as we call the shrubby asters, of which the varieties here are truly elegant; and a wreath of the festoon pine, a pretty evergreen with creeping stalks that run along the ground three or four yards in length, sending up, at the distance of five or six inches, erect, stiff, green stems, resembling some of our heaths in the dark, shining, green, chaffy leaves. The Americans ornament their chimney-glasses with garlands of this plant, mixed with the dried blossoms of the life everlasting; this plant is also called festoonpine. In my rambles in the wood near the house I have discovered a trailing plant bearing a near resemblance to the cedar, which I consider has, with equal propriety, a claim to the name of ground or creeping cedar.

As much of the botany of these unsettled portions of the country is unknown to the naturalist, and the plants are quite nameless, I take the liberty of bestowing names upon them according to inclination or fancy.

My husband has hired people to log up (that is, to draw the chopped timbers into heaps for burning) and clear a space for building our house upon. He has also entered into an agreement with a young settler in our vicinity to complete it for a certain sum within and without, according to a given plan. We are, however, to call the "bee," and provide every thing necessary for the entertainment of our worthy *hive*. Now you know that a "bee," in American language, or rather phraseology, signifies those friendly meetings of neighbours who assemble at your summons to raise the walls of your house, shanty, barn, or any other building: this is termed a "raising bee." Then there are logging-bees, husking-bees, chopping-bees, and quilting-bees. The nature of the work to be done gives the name to the bee. In the more populous and long-settled districts this practice is much discontinued, but it is highly useful, and almost indispensable to new settlers in the remote townships, where the price of labour is proportionately high, and workmen difficult to be procured. . . .

CHAPTER 8 *Settling on the Land*

November the 20th, 1832.

. . . We begin to get reconciled to our Robinson Crusoe sort of life, and the consideration that the present evils are but temporary goes a great way towards reconciling us to them.

One of our greatest inconveniences arises from the badness of our roads, and the distance at which we are placed from any village or town where provisions are to be procured.

Till we raise our own grain and fatten our own hogs, sheep, and poultry, we must be dependent upon the stores for food of every kind. These supplies have to be brought up at considerable expense and loss of time, through our *beautiful bush-roads*; which, to use the words of a poor Irish woman, "can't be no worser." "Och, darlint," she said, "but they are just bad enough, and can't be no worser. Och, but they arn't like our iligant roads in Ireland."

You may send down a list of groceries to be forwarded when a team comes up, and when we examine our stores, behold rice, sugar, currants, pepper, and mustard all jumbled into one mess. What think you of a rice-pudding seasoned plentifully with pepper, mustard, and, maybe, a little rappee or prince's mixture added by way of sauce.

And then woe and destruction to the brittle ware that may chance to travel through our roads. Lucky, indeed, are we if, through the superior carefulness of the person who packs them, more than one-half happens to arrive in safety. For such mishaps we have no redress. The storekeeper lays the accident upon the teamster, and the teamster upon the bad roads, wondering that he himself escapes with whole bones after a journey through the bush.

This is now the worst season of the year—this, and just after the breaking up of the snow. Nothing hardly but an ox-cart can travel along the roads, and even that with difficulty, occupying two days to perform the journey to and fro, and the worst of the matter is, that there are times when the most necessary articles of provisions are not to be procured at any price. You see, then, that a settler in the bush requires to hold himself pretty independent, not only of the luxuries and delicacies of the table, but not unfrequently even of the very necessaries of life.

One time no pork is to be procured; another time there is a scarcity of flour, owing to some accident that has happened to the mill, or for the want of proper supplies of wheat for grinding; or perhaps the weather and bad roads at the same time prevent a team coming up, or people from going down. Then you must have recourse to a neighbour, if you have the good fortune to be near one, or fare the best you can on potatoes. The potato is indeed a great blessing here; new settlers would otherwise be often greatly distressed, and the poor man and his family who are without resources without the potato must starve.

Once our stock of tea was exhausted, and we were unable to

procure more. In this dilemma milk would have been an excellent substitute, or coffee, if we had possessed it; but we had neither the one nor the other, so we agreed to try a Yankee tea—hemlock sprigs boiled. This proved, to my taste, a vile decoction; though I recognized some herb in the tea that was sold in London at five shillings a pound, which I am certain was nothing better than dried hemlock leaves reduced to a coarse powder.

S—— laughed at our wry faces, declaring the potation was excellent; and he set us all an example by drinking six cups of this truly sylvan beverage. . . .

I had reckoned much on the Indian summer, of which I had read such delightful descriptions, but I must say it has fallen far below my expectations. Just at the commencement of this month (November) we experienced three or four warm, hazy days that proved rather close and oppressive. The sun looked red through the misty atmosphere, tinging the fantastic clouds that hung in smoky volumes with saffron and pale crimson light, much as I have seen the clouds above London look on a warm, sultry spring morning through a smoky atmosphere.

Not a breeze ruffled the waters, not a leaf (for the leaves had not entirely fallen) moved. This perfect stagnation of the air was suddenly changed by a hurricane of wind and snow that came on without any previous warning. I was standing near a group of tall pines that had been left in the middle of the clearing, collecting some beautiful crimson lichens, S—— not being many paces distant, with his oxen drawing firewood. Suddenly we heard a distant hollow rushing sound that momentarily increased, the air around us being yet perfectly calm. I looked up, and beheld the clouds, hitherto so motionless, moving with amazing rapidity in several different directions. A dense gloom overspread the heavens. S——, who had been busily engaged with the cattle, had not noticed my being so near, and now called to me to use all the speed I could to gain the house, or an open part of the clearing, distant from the pine-trees. Instinctively I turned towards the house, while the thundering shock of trees falling in all directions at the edge of the forest, the rending of the branches from the pines I had just quitted, and the rush of the whirlwind sweeping down the lake, made me sensible of the danger with which I had been threatened.

The scattered boughs of the pines darkened the air as they

whirled above me; then came the blinding snow-storm: but I could behold the progress of the tempest in safety, having gained the threshold of our house. The driver of the oxen had thrown himself on the ground, while the poor beasts held down their meek heads, patiently abiding "the pelting of the pitiless storm." S——, my husband, and the rest of the household, collected in a group, watched with anxiety the wild havoc of the warring elements. Not a leaf remained on the trees when the hurricane was over; they were bare and desolate. Thus ended the short reign of the Indian summer. It has been supposed by some persons that a great alteration will be effected in this season as the process of clearing the land continues to decrease the quantity of decaying vegetation. Nay, I have heard the difference is already observable by those long acquainted with the American continent....

I must now tell you what my husband is doing on our land. He has let out ten acres to some Irish choppers who have established themselves in the shanty for the winter. They are to receive fourteen dollars per acre for chopping, burning, and fencing in that quantity. The ground is to be perfectly cleared of everything but the stumps: these will taken from seven to nine or ten years to decay; the pine, hemlock, and fir remain much longer. The process of clearing away the stumps is too expensive for new beginners to venture upon, labour being so high that it cannot be appropriated to any but indispensable work. The working season is very short on account of the length of time the frost remains on the ground. With the exception of chopping trees, very little can be done. Those that understand the proper management of uncleared land, usually underbrush (that is, cut down all the small timbers and brushwood), while the leaf is yet on them; this is piled in heaps, and the windfallen trees are chopped through in lengths, to be logged up in the spring with the winter's chopping. The latter end of the summer and the autumn are the best seasons for this work. The leaves then become quite dry and sear, and greatly assist in the important busines of burning off the heavy timbers. Another reason is, that when the snow has fallen to some depth, the light timbers cannot be cut close to the ground, or the dead branches and other incumbrances collected and thrown in heaps.

We shall have about three acres ready for spring crops, provided we get a good burning of that which is already chopped near the site of the house—this will be sown with oats, pumpkins, Indian corn, and potatoes: the other ten acres will be ready for putting in a crop of wheat. So you see it will be a long time before we reap a harvest. We could not even get in spring-wheat early enough to come to perfection this year.

We shall try to get two cows in the spring, as they are little expense during the spring, summer, and autumn; and by the winter we shall have pumpkins and oat-straw for them.

CHAPTER 9 *Building a Log-House*

Lake House, April 18, 1833.

But it is time that I should give you some account of our log-house, into which we moved a few days before Christmas. Many unlooked-for delays having hindered its completion before that time, I began to think it would never be habitable.

The first misfortune that happened was the loss of a fine yoke of oxen that were purchased to draw in the house-logs, that is, the logs for raising the walls of the house. Not regarding the bush as pleasant as their former master's cleared pastures, or perhaps foreseeing some hard work to come, early one morning they took into their heads to ford the lake at the head of the rapids, and march off, leaving no trace of their route excepting their footing at the water's edge. After many days spent in vain search for them, the work was at a stand, and for one month they were gone, and we began to give up all expectation of hearing any news of them. At last we learned they were some twenty miles off, in a distant township, having made their way through bush and swamp, creek and lake, back to their former owner, with an instinct that supplied to them the want of roads and compass.

Oxen have been known to traverse a tract of wild country to a distance of thirty or forty miles going in a direct line for their former haunts by unknown paths, where memory could not avail them. In the dog we consider it is scent as well as memory that guides him to his far-off home—but how is this conduct of the oxen to be accounted for? They returned home through the mazes of interminable forest, where man, with all his reason and knowledge, would have been bewildered and lost.

It was the latter end of October before even the walls of our house were up. To effect this we called "a bee." Sixteen of our neighbours cheerfully obeyed our summons; and though the day was far from favourable, so faithfully did our hive perform their tasks, that by night the outer walls were raised.

The work went merrily on with the help of plenty of Canadian nectar (whiskey), the honey that our *bees* are solaced with. Some huge joints of salt pork, a peck of potatoes, with a rice-pudding, and a loaf as big as an enormous Cheshire cheese, formed the feast that was to regale them during the raising. This was spread out in the shanty, in a *very rural style*. In short, we laughed, and called it a *picnic in the backwoods*; and rude as was the fare, I can assure you, great was the satisfaction expressed by all the guests of every degree, our "bee" being considered as very well conducted. In spite of the difference of rank among those that assisted at the bee, the greatest possible harmony prevailed, and the party separated well pleased with the day's work and entertainment.

The following day I went to survey the newly raised edifice, but was sorely puzzled, as it presented very little appearance of a house. It was merely an oblong square of logs raised one above the other, with open spaces between every row of logs. The spaces for the doors and windows were not then sawn out, and the rafters were not up. In short, it looked a very queer sort of a place, and I returned home a little disappointed, and wondering that my husband should be so well pleased with the progress that had been made. A day or two after this I again visited it. The *sleepers* were laid to support the floors, and the places for the doors and windows cut out of the solid timbers, so that it had not quite so much the look of a bird-cage as before.

After the roof was shingled, we were again at a stand, as no boards could be procured nearer than Peterborough, a long day's journey through horrible roads. At that time no saw-mill was in progress; now there is a fine one building within a little distance of us. Our flooring-boards were all to be sawn by hand, and it was some time before any one could be found to perform this necessary work, and that at high wages—six-and-sixpence per day. Well, the boards were at length down, but of course of unseasoned timber: this was unavoidable; so as they could not be planed we were obliged to put up with their rough, unsightly appearance, for no better were to be had. I began to recall to mind the observation of the old gentleman with whom we travelled from Cobourg to Rice Lake. We console ourselves with the prospect that by next summer the boards will all be seasoned, and then the house is to be turned topsy-turvy by having the floors all relaid, jointed, and smoothed.

The next misfortune that happened was that the mixture of clay and lime that was to plaster the inside and outside of the house between the chinks of the logs was one night frozen to stone. Just as the work was about half completed, the frost suddenly setting in, put a stop to our proceeding for some time, as the frozen plaster yielded neither to fire nor to hot water, the latter freezing before it had any effect on the mass, and rather making bad worse. Then the workman that was hewing the inside walls to smooth them wounded himself with the broad axe, and was unable to resume his work for some time. . . .

Every man in this country is his own glazier; this you will laugh at: but if he does not wish to see and feel the discomfort of broken panes, he must learn to put them in his windows with his own hands. Workmen are not easily to be had in the backwoods when you want them, and it would be preposterous to hire a man at high wages to make two days' journey to and from the nearest town to mend your windows. Boxes of glass of several different sizes are to be bought at a very cheap rate in the stores. My husband employed himself by glazing the windows of the house preparatory to their being put in. . . .

But while I have been recounting these remarks, I have wandered far from my original subject, and left my poor log-house quite in an unfinished state. At last I was told it was in a habitable condition, and I was soon engaged in all the bustle and fatigue attendant on removing our household goods. We received all the assistance we required from S——, who is ever ready and willing to help us. He laughed, and called it a "*moving* bee"; I said it was a "fixing bee"; and my husband said it was a "settling bee." I know we were unsettled enough till it was over. What a den of desolation is a small house, or any house under such circumstances. The idea of chaos must have been taken from a removal or a settling to rights, for I suppose the ancients had their *flitting*, as the Scotch call it, as well as the moderns.

Various were the valuable articles of crockeryware that perished in their short but rough journey through the woods. Peace to their manes. I had a good helper in my Irish maid, who soon roused up famous fires and set the house in order.

We have now got quite comfortably settled, and I shall give you a description of our little dwelling. The part finished is only a portion of the original plan; the rest must be added next spring, or fall, as circumstances may suit.

A nice small sitting-room with a store closet, a kitchen, pantry, and bed-chamber form the ground floor; there is a good upper floor that will make three sleeping-rooms.

'What a nut-shell!' I think I hear you exclaim. So it is at present; but we purpose adding a handsome frame front as soon as we can get boards from the mill, which will give us another parlour, long hall, and good spare bed-room. The windows and glass door of our present sitting-room command pleasant lake-views to the west and south. When the house is completed we shall have a verandah in front and at the south side, which forms an agreeable addition in the summer, being used as a sort of outer room, in which we can dine, and have the advantage of cool air, protected from the glare of the sunbeams. The Canadians call these verandahs "stoups." Few houses, either log or frame, are without them. The pillars look extremely pretty, wreathed with the luxuriant hop-vine, mixed with the scarlet creeper and *"morning glory,"* (the American name for the most splendid of major convolvuluses.) These stoups are really a considerable ornament, as they conceal in a great measure the rough logs, and break the barn-like form of the buildings.

Our parlour is warmed by a handsome Franklin stove with brass gallery and fender. Our furniture consists of a brass-railed sofa, which serves upon occasion for a bed; Canadian painted chairs; a stained pine table; green and white muslin curtains; and a handsome Indian mat which covers the floor. One side of the room is filled up with our books. Some large maps and a few good prints nearly conceal the rough walls, and form the decoration of our little dwelling. Our bed-chamber is furnished with equal simplicity. We do not, however, lack comfort in our humble home; and though it is not exactly such as we could wish, it is as good as, under existing circumstances, we could expect to obtain.

I am anxiously looking forward to the spring, that I may get a garden laid out in front of the house; as I mean to cultivate some of the native fruits and flowers, which, I am sure, will improve greatly by culture. The strawberries that grow wild in our pastures, woods, and clearings, are of two varieties, and bear abundantly. They make excellent preserves, and I mean to introduce beds of them into my garden. There is a pretty little wooded islet on our lake, that is called Strawberry Island, another Raspberry Island; they abound in a variety of fruits—wild grapes, raspberries, strawberries, black and red currants, a wild gooseberry, and a beautiful little trailing plant that bears white flowers like the raspberry and a darkish purple fruit consisting of a few grains of a pleasant brisk acid, somewhat like in flavour to our dewberry, only not quite so sweet. The leaves of this plant are of a bright light green, in shape like the raspberry, to which it bears in some respects so great a resemblance (though it is not shrubby or thorny) that I have called it the "trailing raspberry."

I suppose our scientific botanists in Britain would consider me very impertinent in bestowing names on the flowers and plants I meet with in these wild woods: I can only say, I am glad to discover the Canadian or even the Indian names if I can, and where they fail I consider myself free to become their floral godmother, and give them names of my own choosing.

Among our wild fruits we have plums, which, in some townships, are very fine and abundant; these make admirable preserves, especially when boiled in maple molasses, as is done by the American housewives. Wild cherries, also a sort called choke berries, from their peculiar astringent qualities, high and low-bush cranberries, blackberries, which are brought by the squaws in birch baskets—all these are found on the plains and beaver meadows. The low-bush cranberries are brought in great quantities by the Indians to the towns and villages. They form a standing preserve on the tea-tables in most of the settlers' houses; but for richness of flavour, and for beauty of appearance, I admire the high-bush cranberries; these are little sought after, on account of the large flat seeds, which prevent them from being used as a jam; the jelly, however, is delightful, both in colour and flavour.

The bush on which this cranberry grows resembles the guelder rose. The blossoms are pure white, and grow in loose umbels; they are very ornamental, when in bloom, to the woods and swamps skirting the lakes. The berries are rather of a long oval, and of a brilliant scarlet, and when just touched by the frosts are semi-transparent, and look like pendent bunches of scarlet grapes.

I was tempted one fine frosty afternoon to take a walk with my husband on the ice, which I was assured was perfectly safe. I must confess for the first-half mile I felt very timid, especially when the ice is so transparent that you may see every little pebble or weed at the bottom of the water. Sometimes the ice was thick and white, and quite opaque. As we kept within a little distance of the shore, I was struck by the appearance of some splendid red berries on the leafless bushes that hung over the margin of the lake, and soon recognized them to be the aforesaid high-bush cranberries. My husband soon stripped the boughs of their tempting treasure, and I, delighted with my prize, hastened home, and boiled the fruit with some sugar to eat at tea with our cakes. I never ate anything more delicious than they proved; the more so perhaps from having been so long without tasting fruit of any kind, with the exception of preserves, during our journey, and at Peterborough.

Soon after this I made another excursion on the ice, but it was not in quite so sound a state. We nevertheless walked on for about three-quarters of a mile. We were overtaken on our return by S—— with a handsleigh, which is a sort of barrow, such as porters use, without sides, and instead of a wheel, is fixed on wooden runners, which you can drag over the snow and ice with the greatest ease, if ever so heavily laden. S—— insisted that he would draw me home over the ice like a Lapland lady on a sledge. I was soon seated in state, and in another minute felt myself impelled forward with a velocity that nearly took away my breath. By the time we reached the shore I was in a glow from head to foot....

CHAPTER 10 *Winter in Canada*

Lake House, May 9th, 1833.

What a different winter this has been to what I had anticipated. The snows of December were continually thawing; on the 1st of January not a flake was to be seen on our clearing, though it lingered in the bush. The warmth of sun was so great on the first and second days of the new year that it was hardly possible to endure a cloak, or even shawl, out of doors; and within, the fire was quite too much for us. The weather remained pretty open till the latter part of the month, when the cold set in severely enough, and continued so during February. The 1st of March was the coldest day and night I ever experienced in my life; the mercury was down to twenty-five degrees in the house; abroad it was much lower. The sensation of cold early in the morning was very painful, producing an involuntary shuddering, and an almost convulsive feeling in the chest. Our breaths were congealed in hoar-frost on the sheets and blankets. Every thing we touched of metal seemed to freeze our fingers. This excessive degree of cold only lasted three days, and then a gradual amelioration of temperature was felt. The glass was from fifteen degrees to thirty degrees at this time.

During this very cold weather I was surprised by the frequent recurrence of a phenomenon that I suppose was of an electrical nature. When the frosts were most intense I noticed that when I undressed, my clothes, which are at this cold season chiefly of woollen cloth, or lined with flannel, gave out when moved a succession of sounds, like the crackling and snapping of fire, and in the absence of a candle emitted sparks of a pale whitish blue light, similar to the flashes produced by cutting loaf-sugar in the dark, or stroking the back of a black cat; the same effect was also produced when I combed and brushed my hair.

The snow lay very deep on the ground during February, and until the 19th of March, when a rapid thaw commenced, which continued without intermission till the ground was thoroughly freed from its hoary livery, which was effected in less than a fortnight's time. The air during the progress of the thaw was much warmer and more balmy than it usually is in England, when a disagreeable damp cold is felt during that process. . . .

But I must now tell you of our sugar-making, in which I take rather an active part. Our experiment was on a very limited scale, having but one kettle, besides two iron tripods; but it was sufficient to initiate us in the art and mystery of boiling the sap into molasses, and finally the molasses down into sugar.

The first thing to be done in tapping the maples is to provide little rough troughs to catch the sap as it flows: these are merely pieces of pine-tree, hollowed with the axe. The tapping the tree is done by cutting a gash in the bark, or boring a hole with an auger. The former plan, as being most readily performed, is that most usually practised. A slightly-hollowed piece of cedar or elder is then inserted, so as to slant downwards and direct the sap into the trough; I have even seen a flat chip made the conductor. Ours were managed according to rule, you may be sure. The sap runs most freely after a frosty night, followed by a bright warm day; it should be collected during the day in a barrel or large trough, capable of holding all that can be boiled down the same evening; it should not stand more than twenty-four hours, as it is apt to ferment, and will not grain well unless fresh.

My husband, with an Irish lad, began collecting the sap the last week in March. A pole was fixed across two forked stakes, strong enough to bear the weight of the big kettle. Their employment during the day was emptying the troughs and chopping wood to supply the fires. In the evening they lit the fires and began boiling down the sap.

It was a pretty and picturesque sight to see the sugar-boilers, with their bright log-fire among the trees, now stirring up the blazing pile, now throwing in the liquid and stirring it down with a big ladle. When the fire grew fierce, it boiled and foamed up in the kettle, and they had to throw in fresh sap to keep it from running over.

When the sap begins to thicken into molasses it is then brought to the sugar-boiler to be finished. The process is simple; it only requires attention in skimming and keeping the mass from boiling over till it has arrived at the sugaring point, which is ascertained by dropping a little into cold water. When it is near the proper consistency, the kettle or pot becomes full of yellow froth that dimples and rises in large bubbles from beneath. These throw out puffs of steam, and when the molasses is in this stage, it is nearly converted into sugar. Those who pay great attention to keeping the liquid free from scum, and understand the precise sugaring point, will produce an article little if at all inferior to muscovado.

In general you see the maple-sugar in large cakes, like bees' wax, close and compact, without showing the crystallization; but it looks more beautiful when the grain is coarse and sparkling and the sugar is broken in rough masses like sugar-candy.

The sugar is rolled or scraped down with a knife for use, as it takes long to dissolve in the tea without this preparation. I superintended the last part of the process, that of boiling the molasses down to sugar; and, considering it was a first attempt, and without any experienced person to direct me, otherwise than the information I obtained from S——, I succeeded tolerably well, and produced some sugar of a fine sparkling grain and good colour. Besides the sugar, I made about three gallons of molasses, which proved a great comfort to us, forming a nice ingredient in cakes and an excellent sauce for puddings.

With regard to the expediency of making maple-sugar, it depends on circumstances whether it be profitable or not to the farmer. If he have to hire hands for the work, and pay high wages, it certainly does not answer to make it, unless on a large scale. One thing in its favour is that the sugar season commences at a time when little else can be done on the farm, with the exception of chopping, the frost not being sufficiently out of the ground to admit of crops being sown; time is, therefore, less valuable than it is later in the spring.

Where there is a large family of children and a convenient sugar-bush on the lot, the making of sugar and molasses is decidedly a saving; as young children can be employed in emptying the troughs and collecting fire-wood, the bigger ones can tend the kettles and keep up the fire while the sap is boiling, and the wife and daughters can finish off the sugar within-doors.

Maple-sugar sells for four-pence and six-pence per pound, and sometimes for more. At first I did not particularly relish the flavour it gave to tea, but after awhile I liked it far better than muscovado, and as a sweetmeat it is to my taste delicious. I shall send you a specimen by the first opportunity, that you may judge for yourself of its excellence.

The weather is now very warm – oppressively so. We can scarcely endure the heat of the cooking-stove in the kitchen. As to a fire in the parlour, there is not much need of it, as I am glad to sit at the open door and enjoy the lake-breeze. The insects are already beginning to be troublesome, particularly the black flies—a wicked-looking fly, with black body and white legs and wings; you do not feel their bite for a few minutes, but are made aware of it by a stream of blood flowing from the wound; after a few hours the part swells and becomes extremely painful.

These "*beasties*" chiefly delight in biting the sides of the throat, ears, and sides of the cheek, and with me the swelling continues for many days. The mosquitoes are also very annoying. I care more for the noise they make even than their sting. To keep them out of the house we light little heaps of damp chips, the smoke of which drives them away; but this remedy is not entirely effectual, and is of itself rather an annoyance.

This is the fishing season. Our lakes are famous for masquinongé, salmon-trout, whitefish, black bass, and many others. We often see the lighted canoes of the fishermen pass and repass of a dark night before our door. S—— is considered very skilful as a spearsman, and enjoys the sport so much that he seldom misses a night favourable for it. The darker the night and the calmer the water the better it is for the fishing.

It is a very pretty sight to see these little barks slowly stealing from some cove of the dark pine-clad shores, and manœuvring among the islands on the lakes, rendered visible in the darkness by the blaze of light cast on the water from the jack—a sort of open grated iron basket, fixed to a long pole at the bows of the skiff or canoe. This is filled with a very combustible substance called fat-pine, which burns with a fierce and rapid flame, or else with rolls of birch-bark, which is also very easily ignited.

The light from above renders objects distinctly visible below the surface of the water. One person stands up in the middle of the boat with his fish-spear—a sort of iron trident—ready to strike at the fish that he may chance to see gliding in the still waters, while another with his paddle steers the canoe cautiously along. This sport requires a quick eye, a steady hand, and great caution in those that pursue it.

I delight in watching these torch-lighted canoes so quietly gliding over the calm waters, which are illuminated for yards with a bright track of light, by which we may distinctly perceive the figure of the spearsman standing in the centre of the boat, first glancing to one side, then the other, or poising his weapon ready for a blow. When four or five of these lighted vessels are seen at once on the fishing-ground, the effect is striking and splendid.

The Indians are very expert in this kind of fishing; the squaws paddling the canoes with admirable skill and dexterity. There is another mode of fishing in which these people also excel: this is fishing on the ice when the lakes are frozen over—a sport that requires the exercise of great patience. The Indian, provided with his tomahawk, with which he makes an opening in the ice, a spear, his blanket, and a decoy-fish of tin, proceeds to the place he has fixed upon. Having cut a hole in the ice he places himself on hands and knees, and casts his blanket over him so as to darken the water and conceal himself from observation; in this position he will remain for hours, patiently watching the approach of his prey, which he strikes with admirable precision as soon as it appears within the reach of his spear.

The masquinongé thus caught are superior in flavour to those taken later in the season, and may be bought very reasonably from the Indians. I gave a small loaf of bread for a fish weigheing from eighteen to twenty pounds. The masquinongé is to all appearance a large species of the pike, and possesses the ravenous propensities of that fish.

One of the small lakes of the Otonabee is called Trout Lake, from the abundance of salmon-trout that occupy its waters. The whitefish is also found in these lakes and is very delicious. The large sorts of fish are mostly taken with the spear, few persons having time for angling in this busy country.

As soon as the ice breaks up, our lakes are visited by innumerable flights of wild-fowl: some of the ducks are extremely beautiful in their plumage, and are very fine-flavoured. I love to watch these pretty creatures, floating so tranquilly on the water, or suddenly rising and skimming along the edge of the pine-fringed shores, to drop again on the surface, and then remain stationary, like a little fleet at anchor. Sometimes we see an old duck lead out a brood of little ones from among the rushes; the innocent, soft things look very pretty, sailing round their mother, but at the least appearance of danger they disappear instantly by diving. The frogs are great enemies to the young broods; they are also the prey of the masquinongé, and, I believe, of other large fish that abound in these waters.

The ducks are in the finest order during the early part of the summer, when they resort to the rice-beds in vast numbers, getting very fat on the green rice, which they eagerly devour.

The Indians are very successful in their duck-shooting; they fill a canoe with green boughs, so that it resembles a sort of floating island; beneath the cover of these boughs they remain concealed, and are enabled by this device to approach much nearer than they otherwise could do to the wary birds. The same plan is often adopted by our own sportsmen with great success....

CHAPTER II *Clearing the Land*

November the 2nd, 1833.

Many thanks, dearest mother, for the contents of the box which arived in August. I was charmed with the pretty caps and worked frocks sent for my baby; the little fellow looks delightful in his new robes, and I can almost fancy is conscious of the accession to his wardrobe, so proud he seems of his dress. He grows fat and lively, and, as you may easily suppose, is at once the pride and delight of his foolish mother's heart.

His father, who loves him as much as I do myself, often laughs at my fondness, and asks me if I do not think him the ninth wonder of the world. He has fitted up a sort of rude carriage on the hand-sleigh for the little fellow—nothing better than a tea-chest, lined with a black bear-skin, and in this humble equipage he enjoys many a pleasant ride over the frozen ground.

Nothing could have happened more opportunely for us than the acquisition of my uncle's legacy, as it has enabled us to make some useful additions to our farm, for which we must have waited a few years. We have laid out a part of the property in purchasing a fine lot of land adjoining our home lot. The quality of our new purchase is excellent, and, from its situation, greatly enhances the value of the whole property.

We had a glorious burning this summer after the ground vas all logged up; that is, all the large timbers chopped into engths, and drawn together in heaps with oxen. To effect this he more readily we called a logging-bee. We had a number of ettlers attend, with yokes of oxen and men to assist us. After hat was over, my husband, with the menservants, set the eaps on fire; and a magnificent sight it was to see such a con-lagration all round us. I was a little nervous at first on account f the nearness of some of the log-heaps to the house, but care s always taken to fire them with the wind blowing in a irection away from the building. Accidents have sometimes appened, but they are of rarer occurrence than might be ex-ected when we consider the subtlety and destructiveness of he element employed on the occasion.

If the weather be very dry, and a brisk wind blowing, the vork of destruction proceeds with astonishing rapidity; some-imes the fire will communicate with the forest and run over nany hundreds of acres. This is not considered favourable for learing, as it destroys the underbrush and light timbers, which re almost indispensable for ensuring a good burning. It is, owever, a magnificent sight to see the blazing trees and watch he awful progress of the conflagration, as it hurries onward, onsuming all before it, or leaving such scorching mementos s have blasted the forest growth for years.

When the ground is very dry the fire will run all over the allow, consuming the dried leaves, sticks, and roots. Of a ight the effect is more evident; sometimes the wind blows articles of the burning fuel into the hollow pines and tall ecaying stumps; these readily ignite, and after a time present n appearance that is exceedingly fine and fanciful. Fiery olumns, the bases of which are hidden by the dense smoke vreaths, are to be seen in every direction, sending up showers f sparks that are whirled about like rockets and fire-wheels n the wind. Some of these tall stumps, when the fire has eached the summit, look like gas lamps newly lit. The fire will ometimes continue unextinguished for days.

After the burning is over the brands are collected and drawn ogether again to be reburnt; and, strange as it may appear to ou, there is no work that is more interesting and exciting than hat of tending the log-heaps, rousing up the dying flames and losing them in, and supplying the fires with fresh fuel.

There are always two burnings: first, the brush heaps, which have lain during the winter till the drying winds and hot suns of April and May have rendered them sear, are set fire to; this is previous to forming the log-heaps.

If the season be dry, and a brisk wind abroad, much of the lighter timber is consumed, and the larger trees reduced during this first burning. After this is over, the rest is chopped and logged up for the second burning: and lastly, the remnants are collected and consumed till the ground be perfectly free from all encumbrances, excepting the standing stumps, which rarely burn out, and remain eye-sores for several years. The ashes are then scattered abroad, and the field fenced in with split timbers; the great work of clearing is over.

Our crops this year are oats, corn, and pumpkins, and potatoes, with some turnips. We shall have wheat, rye, oats, potatoes and corn next harvest, which will enable us to increase our stock. At present we have only a yoke of oxen. (Buck and Bright, the names of three-fourths of all the working oxen in Canada), two cows, two calves, three small pigs, ten hens, and three ducks, and a pretty brown pony: but she is such a skilful clearer of seven-railed fences that we shall be obliged to part with her. *Breachy* cattle of any kind are great disturbers of public tranquillity and private friendship; for which reason any settler who values the good will of his neighbours would rather part with the best working yoke of oxen in the township than keep them if they prove *breachy*.

A small farmer at home would think very poorly of our Canadian possessions, especially when I add that our whole stock of farming implements consists of two reaping-hooks, several axes, a spade, and a couple of hoes. Add to these a queer sort of harrow that is made in the shape of a triangle for the better passing between the stumps: this is a rude machine compared with the nicely painted instruments of the sort I have been accustomed to see used in Britain. It is roughly hewn, and put together without regard to neatness; strength for use is all that is looked to here. The plough is seldom put into the land before the third or fourth year, nor is it required; the general plan of cropping the first fallow with wheat or oats, and sowing grass-seeds with the grain to make pastures renders the plough unnecessary till such time as the grass lands require to be broken up. This method is pursued by most settlers while they are clearing bush-land; always chopping and burning enough to keep a regular succession of wheat and spring crops, while the former clearings are allowed to remain in grass. . . .

On first coming to this country nothing surprised me more than the total absence of trees about the dwelling-houses and cleared lands; the axe of the chopper relentlessly levels all before him. Man appears to contend with the trees of the forest as though they were his most obnoxious enemies; for he spares neither the young sapling in its greenness nor the ancient trunk in its lofty pride; he wages war against the forest with fire and steel.

There are several sufficient reasons to be given for this seeming want of taste. The forest-trees grow so thickly together that they have no room for expanding and putting forth lateral branches; on the contrary, they run up to an amazing height of stem, resembling seedlings on a hot-bed that have not duly been thinned out. Trees of this growth when unsupported by others are tall, weak, and entirely divested of those graces and charms of outline and foliage that would make them desirable as ornaments to our grounds; but this is not the most cogent reason for not leaving them, supposing some more sightly than others were to be found.

Instead of striking deep roots in the earth, the forest-trees, with the exception of the pines, have very superficial hold in the earth; the roots running along the surface have no power to resist the wind when it bends the tops, which thus acts as a powerful lever in tearing them from their places.

The taller the tree the more liable it is to being uprooted by storms; and if those that are hemmed in, as in thickly-planted forests, fall, you may suppose the certain fate of any isolated tree, deprived of its former protectors, when left to brave the battle with the storm. It is sure to fall, and may chance to injure any cattle that are within its reach. This is the great reason why trees are not left in the clearing. Indeed, it is a less easy matter to spare them when chopping than I at first imagined, but the fall of one tree frequently brings down two, three, or even more smaller ones that stand near it. A good chopper will endeavour to promote this as much as possible by partly chopping through smaller ones in the direction they purpose the larger one to fall.

I was so desirous of preserving a few pretty sapling beech-trees that pleased me that I desired the choppers to spare them; but the only one that was saved from destruction in the chopping had to pass through a fiery ordeal, which quickly scorched and withered up its gay green leaves: it now stands a melancholy monument of the impossibility of preserving trees thus left. The only thing to be done if you desire trees is to plant them while young in favourable situations, when they take deep root and spread forth branches the same as the trees in our parks and hedgerows.

Another plan which we mean to adopt on our land is to leave several acres of forest in a convenient situation, and chop and draw out the old timbers for firewood, leaving the younger growth for ornament. This method of preserving a grove of trees is not liable to the objections formerly stated, and combines the useful with the ornamental....

CHAPTER 12 *Indian Neighbours*

Lake Cottage, March 14, 1834.

You say you fear the rigours of the Canadian winter will kill me. I never enjoyed better health, nor so good, as since it commenced. There is a degree of spirit and vigour infused into one's blood by the purity of the air that is quite exhilarating. The very snow seems whiter and more beautiful than it does in your damp, vapoury climate. During a keen bright winter's day you will often perceive the air filled with minute frozen particles, which are quite dry, and slightly prick your face like needle-points, while the sky is blue and bright above you. There is a decided difference between the first snow-falls and those of mid-winter; the first are in large soft flakes, and seldom remain long without thawing, but those that fall after the cold has regularly set in are smaller, drier, and of the most beautiful forms, sometimes pointed like a cluster of rays, or else feathered in the most exquisite manner.

I find my eyes much inconvenienced by the dazzling glitter of the snow on bright sunny days, so as to render my sight extremely dull and indistinct for hours after exposure to its power. I would strongly advise any one coming out to this country to provide themselves with blue or green glasses; and by no means to omit green crapé or green tissue veils.

. . . Feeling some desire to see these singular people in their winter encampment, I expressed my wish to S——, who happens to be a grand favourite with the old hunter and his family; as a mark of a distinction they have bestowed on him the title of Chippewa, the name of their tribe. He was delighted with the opportunity of doing the honours of the Indian wigwam, and it was agreed that he, with some of his brothers and sisters-in-law, who happened to be on a visit at his house, should come and drink tea with us and accompany us to the camp in the woods.

A merry party we were that sallied forth that evening into the glorious starlight; the snow sparkled with a thousand diamonds on its frozen surface, over which we bounded with hearts as light as hearts could be in this careful world. And truly never did I look upon a lovelier sight than the woods presented; there had been a heavy fall of snow the preceding day; owing to the extreme stillness of the air not a particle of it had been shaken from the trees. The evergreens were bending beneath their brilliant burden; every twig, every leaf, and spray was covered, and some of the weak saplings actually bowed down to the earth with the weight of snow, forming the most lovely and fanciful bowers and arcades across our path. As you looked up towards the tops of the trees the snowy branches seen against the deep blue sky formed a silvery veil, through which the bright stars were gleaming with a chastened brilliancy.

I was always an admirer of a snowy landscape, but neither in this country nor at home did I ever see any thing so surprisingly lovely as the forest appeared that night.

Leaving the road we struck into a by-path, deep tracked by the Indians, and soon perceived the wigwam by the red smoke that issued from the open basket-work top of the little hut. This is first formed with light poles, planted round so as to enclose a circle of ten or twelve feet in diameter; between these poles are drawn large sheets of birch-bark both within and without, leaving an opening of the bare poles at the top so as to form an outlet for the smoke; the outer walls were also banked up with snow, so as to exclude the air entirely from beneath.

Some of our party, who were younger and lighter of foot than we sober married folks, ran on before; so that when the blanket that served the purpose of a door was unfastened, we found a motley group of the dark skins and the pale faces reposing on the blankets and skins that were spread round the walls of the wigwam.

The swarthy complexions, shaggy black hair and singular costume of the Indians formed a striking contrast with the fair-faced Europeans that were mingled with them, seen as they were by the red and fitful glare of the wood-fire that occupied the centre of the circle. The deer-hounds lay stretched in indolent enjoyment, close to the embers, while three or four dark-skinned little urchins were playing with each other, or angrily screaming out their indignation against the apish tricks of the hunchback, my old acquaintance Maquin, that Indian Flibberty-gibbet, whose delight appeared to be in teazing and tormenting the little papooses, casting as he did so sidelong glances of impish glee at the guests, while as quick as thought his features assumed an impenetrable gravity when the eyes of his father or the squaws seemed directed towards his tricks.

There was a slight bustle among the party when we entered one by one through the low blanket-doorway. The merry laugh rang round among our friends, which was echoed by more than one of the Indian men, and joined by the peculiar half-laugh or chuckle of the squaws. "*Chippewa*" was directed to a post of honour beside the hunter Peter; and squaw Peter, with an air of great good humour, made room for me on a corner of her own blanket; to effect which two papooses and a hound were sent lamenting to the neighbourhood of the hunchback Maquin.

The most attractive persons in the wigwam were two Indian girls, one about eighteen—Jane, the hunter's eldest daughter, and her cousin Margaret. I was greatly struck with the beauty of Jane; her features were positively fine, and though of gipsey darkness the tint of vermilion on her cheek and lip rendered it, if not beautiful, very attractive. Her hair, which was of jetty blackness, was soft and shining, and was neatly folded over her forehead, not hanging loose and disorderly in shaggy masses, as is generally the case with the squaws. Jane was evidently aware of her superior charms, and may be considered as an Indian belle by the peculiar care she displayed in the arrangement of the black cloth mantle, bound with scarlet, that was gracefully wrapped over one shoulder, and fastened at her left side with a gilt brooch. Margaret was younger, of lower stature, and though lively and rather pretty, yet wanted the quiet dignity of her cousin; she had more of the squaw in face and figure. The two girls occupied a blanket by themselves, and were busily engaged in working some most elegant sheaths of deer-skin, richly wrought over with coloured quills and beads: they kept the beads and quills in a small tin baking-pan on their knees; but my old squaw (as I always call Mrs Peter) held her porcupine-quills in her mouth, and the fine dried sinews of the deer, which they make use of instead of thread in work of this sort, in her bosom.

On my expressing a desire to have some of the porcupine-quills, she gave me a few of different colour that she was working a pair of moccasins with, but signified that she wanted "'*bead*' to work mocsin," by which I understood I was to give some in exchange for the quills. Indians never give since they have learned to trade with white men.

She was greatly delighted with the praises I bestowed on Jane. She told me Jane was soon to marry the young Indian who sat on one side of her in all the pride of a new blanket coat, red sash, embroidered powder-pouch, and great gilt clasps to the collar of his coat, which looked as warm and as white as a newly washed fleece. The old squaw evidently felt proud of the young couple as she gazed on them, and often repeated, with a good-tempered laugh, "Jane's husband—marry by and by."

We had so often listened with pleasure to the Indians singing their hymns of a Sunday night that I requested some of them to sing to us; the old hunter nodded assent; and, without removing his pipe, with the gravity and phlegm of a Dutchman, issued his commands, which were as instantly obeyed by the younger part of the community, and a chorus of rich voices filled the little hut with a melody that thrilled to our very hearts.

The hymn was sung in the Indian tongue, a language that is peculiarly sweet and soft in its cadences, and seems to be composed with many vowels. I could not but notice the modest air of the girls; as if anxious to avoid observation that they felt was attracted by their sweet voices, they turned away from the gaze of the strangers, facing each other and bending their heads down over the work they still held in their hands. The attitude, which is that of the Eastern nations; the dress, dark hair and eyes, the olive complexion, heightened colour, and meek expression of face, would have formed a study for a painter. I wish you could have witnessed the scene; I think you would not easily have forgotten it. I was pleased with the air of deep reverence that sat on the faces of the elders of the Indian family as they listened to the voices of their children singing praise and glory to the God and Saviour they had learned to fear and love.

The Indians seem most tender parents; it is pleasing to see the affectionate manner in which they treat their young children, fondly and gently caressing them with eyes overflowing and looks of love. During the singing each papoose crept to the feet of its respective father and mother, and those that were too young to join their voices to the little choir, remained quite silent till the hymn was at an end. One little girl, a fat brown roly-poly, of three years old, beat time on her father's knee, and from time to time chimed in her infant voice; she evidently possessed a fine ear and natural taste for music.

I was at a loss to conceive where the Indians kept their stores, and clothes and other moveables, the wigwam being so small that there seemed no room for anything besides themselves and their hounds. Their ingenuity, however, supplied the want of room, and I soon discovered a plan that answered all the purposes of closets, bags, boxes, etc., the inner lining of birch-bark being drawn between the poles so as to form hollow pouches all round; in these pouches were stowed their goods; one set held their stock of dried deer's flesh, another dried fish, a third contained some flat cakes, which I have been told they bake in a way peculiar to themselves, with hot ashes over and under; for my part I think they must be far from palatable so seasoned. Their dressed skins, clothes, materials for their various toys, such as beads, quills, bits of cloth, silk, with a thousand other miscellaneous articles, occupied the rest of these reservoirs.

Though open for a considerable space at the top, the interior of the wigwam was so hot I could scarcely breathe, and was constrained to throw off all my wrappings during the time we stayed. Before we went away the hunter insisted on showing us a game, which was something after the manner of our cup and ball, only more complicated, and requires more sleight of hand; the Indians seemed evidently well pleased at our want of adroitness. They also showed us another game, which was a little like nine-pins, only the number of sticks stuck in the ground was greater. I was unable to stay to see the little rows of sticks knocked out, as the heat of the wigwam oppressed me almost to suffocation, and I was glad to feel myself once more breathing the pure air.

In any other climate one would scarcely have undergone such sudden extremes of temperature without catching a severe cold; but fortunately that distressing complaint *catchée le cold*, as the Frenchman termed it, is not so prevalent in Canada as at home....

CHAPTER 13 *Canadian Wild Flowers*

July 13, 1834.

Our winter broke up unusually early this year: by the end of February the ground was quite free from snow, and the weather continued all through March mild and pleasant, though not so warm as the preceding year, and certainly more variable. By the last week in April and the beginning of May, the forest-trees had all burst into leaf, with a brilliancy of green that was exquisitely lovely.

On the 14th, 15th, and 16th of May, the air became suddenly cold, with sharp winds from the north-west, and heavy storms of snow that nipped the young buds and destroyed many of the early-sown vegetable seeds; fortunately for us we were behind-hand with ours, which was very well as it happened.

Our woods and clearings are now full of beautiful flowers. You will be able to form some idea of them from the dried specimens that I send you. You will recognize among them many of the cherished pets of our gardens and green-houses, which are here flung carelessly from Nature's lavish hand among our woods and wilds.

How often do I wish you were beside me in my rambles among the woods and clearings: you would be so delighted in searching out the floral treasures of the place.

Deeply do I now regret having so idly neglected your kind offers while at home of instructing me in flower-painting; you often told me the time would come when I should have cause to regret neglecting the golden opportunity before me.

You proved a true prophetess; for I daily lament that I cannot make faithful representations of the flowers of my adopted country, or understand as you would do their botanical arrangement. With some few I have made myself acquainted, but have hardly confidence in my scanty stock of knowledge to venture on scientific descriptions, when I feel conscious that a blunder would be easily detected, and expose me to ridicule and contempt for an assumption of knowledge that I did not possess. The only botanical work I have at my command is Pursh's North American Flora, from which I have obtained some information; but must confess it is tiresome blundering out Latin descriptions to one who knows nothing of Latin beyond what she derives through a knowledge of Italian.

I have made out a list of the plants most worthy of attention near us; there are many others in the township that I am a stranger to; some there are with whose names I am unacquainted. I subjoin a slight sketch, not with my pencil but my pen, of those flowers that pleased me particularly, or that possessed any remarkable qualities.

The same plants do not grow on cleared land that formerly occupied the same spot when it was covered with forest-trees. A distinct class of vegetation makes its appearance as soon as the fire has passed over the ground.

The same thing may be remarked with regard to the change that takes place among our forests. As one generation falls and decays, new ones of a different character spring up in their places. This is illustrated in the circumstance of the resinous substance called fat-pine being usually found in places where the living pine is least abundant, and where the ground is occupied by oak, ash, beech, maple, and basswood.

The fire-weed, a species of tall thistle of rank and unpleasant scent, is the first plant that appears when the ground has been freed from timbers by fire: if a piece of land lies untilled the first summer after its being chopped, the following spring shows you a smothering crop of this vile weed. The next plant you notice is the sumach, with its downy stalks, and head of deep crimson velvety flowers, forming an upright obtuse bunch at the extremity of the branches: the leaves turn scarlet towards the latter end of the summer. This shrub, though really very ornamental, is regarded as a great pest in old clearings, where the roots run and send up suckers in abundance. The raspberry and wild gooseberry are next seen, and thousands of strawberry plants of different varieties carpet the ground, and mingle with the grasses of the pastures. I have been obliged this spring to root out with remorseless hand hundreds of sarsaparilla plants, and also the celebrated ginseng, which grows abundantly in our woods: it used formerly to be an article of export to China from the States, the root being held in high estimation by the Chinese.

Last week I noticed a succulent plant that made its appearance on a dry sandy path in my garden; it seems to me a variety of the hour-blowing mesembryanthium. It has increased so rapidly that it already covers a large space; the branches converging from the centre of the plant, and sending forth shoots from every joint. The leaves are rather small, three-sided and pointed, thick and juicy, yielding a green liquor when bruised like the common sedums. The stalks are thick and round, of a bright red, and trail along the ground; the leaves spring from each joint, and with them a constant succession of yellow starry flowers, that close in an hour or so from the time they first unfold. I shall send you some of the seed of this plant, as I perceived a number of little green pods that looked like the buds, but which, on opening, proved to be the seed-vessels. This plant covers the earth like a thick mat, and, I am told, is rather troublesome where it likes the soil.

I regret that among my dried plants I could not preserve some specimens of our superb water-lilies and irises; but they were too large and too juicy to dry well. As I cannot send you my favourites, I must describe them to you.

The first, then, is a magnificent water-lily, that I have called by way of distinction the "Queen of the Lakes," for she sits a crown upon the waters. This magnificent flower is about the size of a large dahlia; it is double to the heart: every row of petals diminishing by degrees in size, and gradually deepening in tint from the purest white to the brightest lemon colour. The buds are very lovely, and may be seen below the surface of the water, in different stages of forwardness from the closely-folded bud, wrapped in its olive-green calix, to the half-blown flower, ready to emerge from its watery prison, and in all its virgin beauty expand its snowy bosom to the sun and genial air. Nor is the beauty of the flower its sole attraction: when unfolded it gives out a rich perfume not unlike the smell of fresh lemons. The leaves are also worthy of attention: at first they are of a fine dark green, but as the flower decays the leaf changes its hue to a vivid crimson. Where a large bed of these lilies grow closely together, they give quite a sanguine appearance to the waters, that is distinguishable at some distance.

The yellow species of this plant is also very handsome, though it wants the silken texture and delicate colour of the former; I call this the "Water-king." The flower presents a deep golden-coloured cup, the concave petals of which are clouded in the centre with a dark reddish-brown, which forms a striking contrast to the gay anthers; these are very numerous, and turn back from the centre of the flower, falling like fringes of gold one over the other, in successive rows, till they fill up the hollow flower-cup.

The shallows of our lakes abound with a variety of elegant aquatic plants: I know not a more lovely sight than one of these floating gardens. Here you shall behold near the shore a bed of azure fleur-de-lis, from the palest pearl colour varying to the darkest purple. Nearer in shore, in the shallowest water, the rose-coloured persicaria sends up its beautiful spikes trailing below the surface; you see the red stalks and smooth dark green leaves veined underneath with rosy red: it is a very charming variety of this beautiful species of plants. Then a bed of my favourite white lilies, all in full bloom, floating on the water, with their double flowers expanding to the sun; near these, and rising in stately pride, a tall plant, with dark green spear-shaped leaves, and thick spike of bright blue flowers, is seen. I cannot discover the name of this very grand-looking flower, and I neglected to examine its botanical construction; so can give you no clue by which to discover its name or species.*

* *Pontederia*—Pickerel-weed.

Our rice-beds are far from being unworthy of admiration; seen from a distance they look like low green islands on the lakes: on passing through one of these rice-beds when the rice is in flower, it has a beautiful appearance with its broad grassy leaves and light waving spikes, garnished with pale yellow green blossoms, delicately shaded with reddish purple, from beneath which fall three elegant straw-coloured anthers, which move with every breath of air or slightest motion of the waters. I gathered several spikes when only just opened, but the tiresome things fell to pieces directly they became dry.† Next summer I will make another attempt at preserving them, and it may be with better success.

The low shore of the lake is a complete shrubbery. We have a very pretty St John's-wort, with handsome yellow flowers. The white and pink spiral frutex also abounds with some exquisite upright honeysuckles, shrubby plants about three feet in height; the blossoms grow in pairs or by fours, and hang beneath the light green leaves; elegant trumpet-shaped flowers of a delicate greenish white, which are succeeded by ruby-coloured berries. On gathering a branch of this plant, you cannot but be struck with the elegant arrangement of the flowers along the under part of the stalks. The two blossoms are connected at the nectary of each in a singular manner. The Americans call this honeysuckle "twinflower." I have seen some of the flowers of this plant pale pink; on the whole it is one of the most ornamental shrubs we have. I transplanted some young bushes into my garden last spring; they promise to live and do well. I know it to be a species of honeysuckle(from the class and order, the shape and colour of the leaves, the stalks, the trumpet-shaped blossom and the fruit, all bearing a resemblance to our honeysuckles in some degree. There is a tall upright bush, bearing large yellow trumpet-shaped flowers, springing from the extremities of the branches; the involucrum forms a boat-shaped cup that encircles the flowers from which they seem to spring, something after the manner of the scarlet trumpet-honeysuckle. The leaves and blossoms of this plant are coarse, and by no means to compare to the former.

We have a great variety of curious orchises, some brown and yellow, others pale flesh-coloured, striped with crimson. There

† The Indian rice, as it is called, forms an excellent article of diet. When nicely cooked it is a favourite dish in many families.

is one species grows to the height of two feet, bearing long spikes of pale purple flowers; a white one with most fragrant smell, and a delicate pink one with round head of blossoms, finely fringed like the water-pinks that grow in our marshes; this is a very pretty flower, and grows in the beaver meadows.

Last autumn I observed in the pine-wood near us a very curious plant; it came up with naked brown stems, branching off like some miniature tree; the stalks of this plant were brown, slightly freckled and beset with little knobs. I watched the progress of maturity in this strange plant with some degree of interest, towards the latter end of October; the little knob, which consisted of two angular hard cases, not unlike, when fully opened, to a boat in shape, burst asunder and displayed a pale straw-coloured chaffy substance that resembled fine sawdust: these must have been the anthers, but they bore more resemblance to seeds; this singular flower would have borne examination with a microscope. One peculiarity that I observed was, that on pulling up a plant with its roots, I found the blossoms open under ground, springing up from the lowest part of the flower-stems, and just as far advanced to maturity as those that grew on the upper stalks, excepting that they were somewhat blanched, from being covered up from the air. I can find no description of this plant, nor any person but myself seems to have taken notice of it. The specimen I had on being dried became so brittle that it fell to pieces.*

I have promised to collect some of the most singular of our native flowers for one of the Professors of Botany in the Edinburgh University.

We have a very handsome plant that bears the closest affinity to our potato in its floral construction; it grows to the height of two or three feet in favourable situations, and sends up many branches; the blossoms are large, purely white, freckled near the bottom of the corolla with brownish yellow spots; the corolla is undivided: this is evidently the same plant as the cultivated potato, though it does not appear to form apples at the root. The fruit is very handsome, egg-shaped of a beautiful apricot colour when ripe, and of a shining tempting appearance; the smell, however, betrays its poisonous nature: on opening one of the fruits you find it consists of a soft pulp filled with shining black seeds. The plant continues in blossom from June

* Broom-rape.

till the first frosts wither the leaves; it is far less coarse than the potato; the flower, when full blown, is about the size of a half-crown, and quite flat; I think it is what you call salver-shaped: it delights in light loamy soil, growing on the upturned roots of fallen trees, where the ground is inclined to be sandy. I have never seen this plant elsewhere than on our own fallow.

The hepatica is the first flower of the Canadian spring: it gladdens us with its tints of azure, pink, and white, early in April, soon after the snows have melted from the earth. The Canadians call it snow-flower, from its coming so soon after the snow disappears. We see its gay tufts of flowers in the open clearings and the deep recesses of the forests; its leaves are also an enduring ornament through the open months of the year; you see them on every grassy mound and mossy root; the shades of blue are very various and delicate, the white anthers forming a lovely contrast with the blue petals.

The wood-cress, or as it is called by some, ginger-cress, is a pretty white cruciform flower; it is highly aromatic in flavour; the root is white and fleshy, having the pungency of horse-radish. The leaves are of a sad green, sharply notched, and divided in three lobes; the leaves of some of them are slightly variegated; the plant delights in rich moist vegetable mould, especially on low and slightly swampy ground; the flower-stalk is sometimes naked, sometimes leafed, and is crowned with a loose spike of whitish cruciform flowers.

There is a cress that grows in pretty green tufts at the bottom of the waters in the creeks and small rivulets: it is more delicate and agreeable in flavour than any of the land-cresses; the leaves are of a pale tender green, winged and slender; the plant looks like a green cushion at the bottom of the water. The flowers are yellow, cruciform, and insignificant; it makes a very acceptable salad in the early spring, and at the fall of the year. There are also several species of land-cress, and plants resembling some of the cabbage tribes, that might be used as spring vegetables There are several species of spinach, one known here by the name of lamb's quarter, that grows in great profusion about our garden, and in rich soil rises to two feet, and is very luxuriant in its foliage; the leaves are covered with a white rough powder. The top shoots and tender parts of this vegetable are boiled with pork, and, in place of a more delicate pot-herb, is very useful.

Then we have the Indian turnip; this is a very handsome arum, the leaves of this arum are handsome, slightly tinged with purple. The spathe is of a lively green, striped with purple: the Indians use the root as a medicine. Pursh calls this species *Arum atropurpureum.*

I must not pass over one of our greatest ornaments, the strawberry blite, strawberry-bearing spinach, or Indian strawberry, as it is variously named. This singular plant throws out many branches from one stem; these are garnished with handsome leaves, resembling in appearance our long-leaved garden spinach; the fruit of this plant is of a bright crimson, pulpy like the strawberry, and containing a number of purple seeds, partially embedded in the surface, after the same manner as the strawberry. The fruit grows close to the stalk, completely surrounding it, and forming a long spike of the richest crimson berries. I have gathered branches a foot in length, closely covered with the beautiful-looking fruit, and have regretted that it was so insipid in its flavour as to make it uneatable. On the banks of creeks and in rich ground it grows most luxuriantly, one root sending up twenty or thirty branches, drooping with the weight of their magnificent burden. As the middle and superior stems ripen and decay, the lateral ones come on, presenting a constant succession of fruit from July till the frosts nip them off in September.

The Indians use the juice of this plant as a dye, and are said to eat the berries: it is often made use of as a substitute for red ink, but it is liable to fade unless mingled with alum. A friend of mine told me she had been induced to cross a letter she was sending to a relative in England with this strawberry ink, but not having taken the precaution to fix the colour, when the anxiously expected epistle arrived, one-half of it proved quite unintelligible, the colours having faded nearly to white; so that instead of affording satisfaction, it proved only a source of vexation and embarrassment to the reader, and of mortification to the writer.

The blood-root, *sanguinaria* is worthy of attention from the root to the flower. As soon as the sun of April has warmed the earth and loosened it from its frozen bonds, you may distinguish a number of purely white buds, elevated on a naked footstalk, and partially enfolded in a handsome vine-shaped leaf, of a pale bluish green, curiously veined on the under side with pale orange. The leaf springs singly from a thick juicy fibrous root, which, on being broken, emits a quantity of liquor from its pores of a bright orange scarlet colour: this juice is used by the Indians as a dye, and also in the cure of rheumatic and cutaneous complaints. The flowers of the *sanguinaria* resemble the white crocus very closely; when it first comes up the bud is supported by the leaf, and is folded together with it; the flower, however, soon elevates itself above its protector, while the leaf, having performed its duty of guardian to the tender bud, expands to its full size. A rich black vegetable mould at the edges of the clearings seems the favourite soil for this plant.

The scarlet columbine is another of my favourite flowers; it is bright red, with yellow linings to the tubes. The nectaries are more elongated than in the garden columbines, and form a sort of mural crown, surmounted with little balls at the tips. A tall, graceful plant, with its brilliant waving blossoms, is this columbine; it grows both in the sunshine and the shade, not perhaps in deep shady woods, but where the under brush has been removed by the running of the fire or the axe of the chopper; it seems even to flourish in poor stony soils, and may be found near every dwelling. The feathered columbine delights in moist open swamps and the banks of rivulets; it grows to the height of three, and even four and five feet, and is very ornamental.

Of violets we have every variety of colour, size, and shape, lacking only the delightful *viola odorata* of our home woodlands: yet I know not why we should quarrel with these meek daughters of the spring because they want the fragrance of their more favoured sisters. Many of your wood-violets, though very beautiful, are also devoid of scent; here variety of colour ought to make some amends for want of perfume. We have violets of every shade of blue, some veined with purple, others shaded with darker blue. We have the delicate white, pencilled with purple: the bright brimstone coloured with black veinings: the pale primrose with dark blue veins; the two latter are remarkable for the luxuriance and size of the leaves: the flowers spring in bunches, several from each joint, and are succeeded by large capsules covered with thick white cottony down. There is a species of violet that grows in the woods, the leaves of which are exceedingly large; so are the seed-vessels, but the flower is so small and insignificant that it is only to be observed by a close examination of the plant; this has given rise to the vulgar belief that it blooms underground. The flowers are a pale greenish yellow. Bryant's beautiful poem of the Yellow Violet is descriptive of *viola pubescens.*

There is an elegant *viola tricolor* that blooms in the autumn; it is the size of a small heart's-ease, and is pure white, pale purple, and lilac; the upper petals are white, the lower lip purple, and the side wings a reddish lilac. I was struck with the elegance of this rare flower on a journey to Peterborough, on my way to Cobourg; I was unable to preserve the specimens, and have not travelled that road since. The flower grew among wild clover on the open side of the road; the leaves were small, roundish, and of a dark sad green.

Of the tall shrubby asters we have several beautiful varieties, with large pale blue lilac, or white flowers; others with very small white flowers and crimson anthers, which look like tufts of red down, spangled with gold-dust; these anthers have a pretty effect contrasted with the white starry petals. There is one variety of the tall asters that I have seen on the plains, it has flowers about the size of a sixpence, of a soft pearly tint of blue, with brown anthers; this plant grows very tall, and branches from the parent stem in many graceful flowery boughs; the leaves of this species are of a purple red on the under side, and inclining to heart-shape; the leaves and stalks are hairy.

I am not afraid of wearying you with my floral sketches, I have yet many to describe; among these are those elegant little evergreens that abound in this country, under the name of wintergreens, of which there are three or four remarkable for beauty of foliage, flower, and fruit. One of these wintergreens that abounds in our pine-woods is extremely beautiful; it seldom exceeds six inches in height; the leaves are a bright shining green, of a long narrow oval, delicately notched like the edges of a rose-leaf; and the plant emerges from beneath the snow in the early part of the year, as soon as the first thaw takes place, as fresh and verdant as before they were covered up: it seems to be a shy blossomer. I have never seen specimens of the flowers in bloom but twice; these I carefully preserved for you, but the dried plant will afford but an imperfect idea of the original. You always called, you know, your dried specimens corpses of plants, and said that when well painted their representations were far more like themselves. The flower-stalk rises two or three inches from the centre of the plant, and is crowned with round crimson buds and blossoms, consisting of five petals, deepening from the palest pink to the brightest blush colour; the stigma is of an emerald greenness, forming a slightly ribbed turban in the centre, around which are disposed ten stamens of an amethyst colour: in short, this is one of the gems of the floral world, and might aptly be compared to an emerald ring set round with amethysts. The contrast of colours in this flower is exceedingly pleasing, and the crimson buds and shining evergreen leaves are scarcely less to be admired than the flower itself; it would be considered a great acquisition to your collection of American shrubs, but I doubt if it would flourish when removed from the shade of the pine-woods. This plant appears to be the *Chimaphila corymbosa*, or wintergreen, described by Pursh, with some trifling variation in the colour of the petals.

Another of our wintergreens grows in abundance on the Rice Lake plains; the plant does not exceed four inches; the flowers are in little loose bunches, pale greenish white, in shape like the blossom of the arbutus; the berries are bright scarlet, and are known by the name of winter-berry, and partridge-berry; this must be *Gualtheria procumbens*. But a more beautiful little evergreen of the same species is to be found in our cedar swamps, under the name of pigeon-berry; it resembles the arbutus in leaf and flower more closely than the former plant; the scarlet berry is inserted in a scarlet cup or receptacle, divided at the edge in five points; it is fleshy, seeming to partake of the same nature as the fruit. The blossoms of this elegant little shrub, like the arbutus, of which it looks like the miniature, appear in drooping bunches at the same time the ripened berry of the former year is in perfection; this circumstance adds not a little to the charm of the plant. If I mistake not, this is the *Gualtheria Shallon*, which Pursh likens to the arbutus: this is also one of our wintergreens. An aromatic essence obtained from the leaves of this plant, known as "Spice-Wintergreen," enters largely into the sugar confections sold in the stores.

There is another pretty trailing plant, with delicate little funnel-shaped flowers, and a profusion of small dark green round buds, slightly variegated, and bright red berries, which are produced at the extremities of the branches. The blossoms of this plant grow in pairs, closely connected at the germen; so much so, that the scarlet fruit that supersedes the flowers appears like a double berry, each berry containing the seeds of both flowers and a double eye. The plant is also called winter-green, or twin-berry; it resembles none of the other winter-greens; it grows in mossy woods, trailing along the ground, appearing to delight in covering little hillocks and inequalities of the ground. In elegance of growth, delicacy of flower, and brightness of berry, this wintergreen is little inferior to any of the former. *Mitchella repens*—Partridge-berry.

There is a plant in our woods, known by the names of man-drake, may-apple, and duck-foot: the botanical name of the plant is *Podophyllum*; it belongs to the class and order *Poly-andria monogynia*. The blossom is yellowish white, the corolla consisting of six petals; the fruit is oblong; when ripe, of a greenish yellow; in size that of a plum; when fully ripe it has the flavour of preserved tamarind, a pleasant brisk acid; it increases rapidly in rich moist woodlands. The leaves come up singly, are palmated and shade the ground very much when a number of them grow near each other; the stalk supports the leaf from the centre: when they first appear above the ground, they resemble a folded umbrella or parasol, all the edges of the leaves bending downward, by degrees expanding into a slightly convex canopy. The fruit would make a delicate preserve with sugar.

The lily tribe offer an extensive variety from the most minute to the very largest flowers. The red martagon grows abundantly on our plains; the dog's-tooth violet, *Erythronium*, with its spotted leaves and bending yellow blossoms, delicately dashed with crimson spots within, and marked with fine purple lines on the outer part of the petal, proves a great attraction in our woods, where these plants increase: they form a beautiful bed; the leaves come up singly, one from each separate tuber. There are two varieties of this flower, the pale yellow, with neither spots nor lines, and the deep yellow with both; the anthers of this last are reddish-orange, and thickly covered with a fine powdery substance. The daffodil (*Uvularia perfoliata*—Bell-wort) of our woods is a delicate bending flower, of a pale yellow; its height is from six to eight inches; it delights in the deep shade of moist woods.

A very beautiful plant of the lily tribe abounds both in our woods and clearings; for want of a better name, I call it the

Douro Lily, though it is widely spread over a great portion of the continent. The Americans term the white and red varieties of this species, the "white"* and "red death."† The flower is either deep red, or of a dazzling white, though the latter is often found stained with a delicate blush-pink, or a deep green; the latter appears to be caused by the calix running into the petal. Wherefore it bears so formidable a name has not yet transpired. The flower consists of three petals, the calix three; it belongs to the class and order *Hexandria monogynia*; style, three-cleft; seed-vessel of three valves; soil, dry woods and cleared land; leaves growing in three, springing from the joints, large round, but a little pointed at the extremities. We have lilies of the valley, and the Solomon's seal, also a small flowered Turk's-cap, of pale crimson colour.

Our ferns are very elegant and numerous; I have no less than eight different specimens, gathered from our immediate neighbourhood, some of which are extremely elegant, especially one that I call the "fairy fern,"‡ from its lightness. One elastic stem, of a purplish-red colour, supports several light branches, which are subdivided and furnished with innumerable leafets; each leafet has a footstalk that attaches it to the branch, of so slight and hair-like a substance that the least breath of air sets the whole plant in motion.

Could we but imagine Canada to have been the scene of fairy revels we should declare that these graceful ferns were well suited to shade the elfin court of Oberon and Titania.

When this fern first appears above the ground, it is scarcely to be distinguished from the decaying wood of the fallen pines; it is then of a light reddish brown, curiously curled up. In May and June the leaves unfold, and soon assume the most delicate tint of green; they are almost transparent: the cattle are very fond of this fern.

The moccasin flower or lady's-slipper (mark the odd coincidence between the common name of the American and English species) is one of our most remarkable flowers; both on account of its beauty and its singularity of structure. Our plains and dry sunny pastures produce several varieties; among these, the *Cypripedium pubescens*, or yellow moccasin, and the *C. Arietinum* are the most beautiful of the species. The colour of the

* *Trillium Grandiflorum.* † *Trillium Erectum.*

‡ *Adiantum pedatum.*

lip of the former is a lively canary yellow, dashed with deep crimson spots. The upper petals consist of two short and two long; in texture and colour resembling the sheath of some of the narcissus tribe; the short ones stand erect, like a pair of ears; the long or lateral pair are three times the length of the former, very narrow, and elegantly twisted, like the spiral horns of the Walachian ram: on raising a thick yellow fleshy sort of lid in the middle of the flower, you perceive the exact face of an Indian hound, perfect in all its parts—the eyes, nose, and mouth; below this depends an open sack, slightly gathered round at the opening, which gives it a hollow and prominent appearance; the inside of this bag is delicately dashed with deep crimson spots: the stem of the flower is thick towards the upper part, and takes a direct bend; the leaves are large oval, a little pointed and ribbed; the plant scarcely exceeds six inches: the elegant colour and silken texture of the lower lip or bag renders this flower very much more beautiful to my taste than the purple and white variety, though the latter is much more striking on account of the size of the flower and leaves, besides the contrast between the white and red, or white and purple colours.

The formation of this species resembles the other, only with this difference, the horns are not twisted, and the face is that of a monkey; even the comical expression of the animal is preserved with such admirable fidelity as to draw a smile from everyone that sees the odd restless-looking visage, with its prominent round black eyes peering forth from under its covering.

These plants belong to class and order *Gynandria diandria*; are described with some little variation by Pursh, who, however, likens the face of the latter to that of a sheep: if a sheep sat for the picture methinks it must have been the most mischievous of the flock.

There is a curious aquatic plant that grows in shallow, stagnant, or slow-flowing waters; it will contain a full wine-glass of water. A poor soldier brought it to me, and told me it resembled a plant he used to see in Egypt, that the soldiers called the "Soldier's drinking-cup"; and "many a good draught of pure water," he said, "I have drank from them."

Another specimen was presented me by a gentleman who knew my predilection for strange plants; he very aptly gave it the name of "Pitcher-plant"; it very probably belongs to the tribe that bear that name.

The flowers that afford the most decided perfumes are our wild roses, which possess a delicious scent: the milkweed, which gives out a smell not unlike the night-blowing stock; the purple monarda, which is fragrance itself from the root to the flower, and even after months' exposure to the wintry atmosphere its dried leaves and seed-vessels are so sweet as to impart perfume to your hands or clothes. All our mints are strong scented: the lily of the valley is remarkable for its fine smell; then there is my queen of the lakes; and her consort, the water-king, with many other flowers I cannot now enumerate. Certain it is that among such a vast assemblage of flowers there are, comparatively, very few that are gifted with fragrant scents. Some of our forest-trees give out a fine perfume. I have often paused in my walks to inhale the fragrance from a cedar swamp on some sunny day while the boughs were still wet with the dew-drops or recently fallen shower.

Nor is the balsam-poplar, or tacamahac, less delightfully fragrant, especially while the gummy buds are just beginning to unfold; this is an elegant growing tree where it has room to expand into boughs. It grows chiefly on the shores of the lakes and in open swamps, but it also forms one of the attractions of our plains, with its silver bark and waving foliage; it emits a resinous clear gum in transparent globules on the bark, and the buds are covered with a highly aromatic gummy fluid.

Our grasses are highly interesting; there are varieties that are wholly new to me, and when dried form the most elegant ornaments to our chimney-pieces, and would look very graceful on a lady's head; only fashionists always prefer the artificial to the natural.

One or two species of grass that I have gathered bear a close but of course minute resemblance to the Indian corn, having a top feather and eight-sided spike of little grains disposed at the side-joints. The *sisyrinchium*, or blue-eyed grass, is a pretty little flower of an azure blue, with a golden spot at the base of each petal; the leaves are flat, stiff, and flag-like; this pretty flower grows in tufts on light sandy soils.

I have given you a description of the flowers most worthy of attention; and, though it is very probable some of my descriptions may not be exactly in the technical language of the correct botanist, I have at least described them as they appear.

My dear boy seems already to have a taste for flowers, which I shall encourage as much as possible. It is a study that tends to refine and purify the mind, and can be made, by simple steps, a ladder to heaven, as it were, by teaching a child to look with love and admiration to that bountiful God who created and made flowers so fair to adorn and fructify this earth.

Farewell, my dear sister.

CHAPTER 14 *Canada, the Land of Hope*

September the 20th, 1834.

I promised when I parted from you before I left England to write as soon as I could give you any satisfactory account of our settlement in this country. I shall do my best to redeem that promise, and forward you a slight sketch of our proceedings, with such remarks on the natural features of the place in which we have fixed our abode as I think likely to afford you interest or amusement. Prepare your patience, then, my dear friend, for a long and rambling epistle, in which I may possibly prove somewhat of a Will-o'-the-wisp, and having made you follow me in my desultory wanderings—

Over hill, over dale,
Through bush, through briar,
Over park, over pale,
Through flood, through fire—

possibly leave you in the midst of a big cedar swamp, or among the pathless mazes of our wild woods, without a clue to guide you, or even a *blaze* to light you on your way.

You will have heard, through my letters to my dear mother, of our safe arrival at Quebec, of my illness at Montreal, of all our adventures and misadventures during our journey up the country, till after much weary wandering we finally found a home and resting-place with a kind relative, whom it was our happiness to meet after a separation of many years.

As my husband was anxious to settle in the neighbourhood of one so nearly connected with me, thinking it would rob the woods of some of the loneliness that most women complain so bitterly of, he purchased a lot of land on the shores of a beautiful lake, one of a chain of small lakes belonging to the Otonabee river.

Here, then, we are established, having now some five-and-twenty acres cleared, and a nice house built. Our situation is very agreeable, and each day increases its value. When we first came up to live in the bush, with the exception of S——, there were but two or three settlers near us, and no roads cut. The only road that was available for bringing up goods from the nearest town was on the opposite side of the water, which was obliged to be crossed in a log (known by the expressive name of a dug-out), or birch-bark canoe; the former is nothing better than a large pine-log hollowed with the axe, so as to contain three or four persons; it is flat-bottomed, and very narrow, on which account it is much used on these shallow waters. The birch canoe is made of sheets of birch bark, ingeniously fashioned and sewn together by the Indians with the tough roots of the cedar, young pine, or larch (tamarack, as it is termed by the Indians); it is exceedingly light, so that it can be carried by two persons easily, or even by one. These, then, are our ferry-boats, and very frail they are, and require great nicety in their management; they are worked in the water with paddles, either kneeling or sitting. The squaws are very expert in the management of the canoes, and preserve their balance with admirable skill, while they impel the little bark with great velocity through the water.

Very great is the change that a few years have effected in our situation. A number of highly respectable settlers have purchased land along the shores of these lakes, so that we no longer want society. The roads are now cut several miles above us, and though far from good can be travelled by waggons and sleighs, and are, at all events, better than none.

A village has started up where formerly a thick pine-wood covered the ground; we have now within a short distance of us an excellent saw-mill, a grist-mill, and store, with a large tavern and many good dwellings. A fine timber bridge, on stone piers, was erected last year to connect the opposite townships and lessen the distance to and from Peterborough; and though it was unfortunately swept away early last spring by the unusual rising of the Otonabee lakes, a new and more substantial one has risen upon the ruins of the former, through the activity of an enterprising young Scotchman, the founder of the village.

But the grand work that is, sooner or later, to raise this portion of the district from its present obscurity, is the opening a line of navigation from Lake Huron through Lake Simcoe, and so through our chain of small lakes to Rice Lake, and finally through the Trent to the Bay of Quinte. This noble work would prove of incalculable advantage, by opening a direct communication between Lake Huron and the inland townships at the back of the Ontario with the St Laurence. This project has already been under the consideration of the Governor, and is at present exciting great interest in the country: sooner or later there is little doubt but that it will be carried into effect. It presents some difficulties and expense, but it would be greatly to the advantage and prosperity of the country, and be the means of settling many of the back townships bordering upon these lakes.

I must leave it to abler persons than myself to discuss at large the policy and expediency of the measure; but as I suppose you have no intention of emigrating to our backwoods, you will be contented with my cursory view of the matter, and believe, as in friendship you are bound to do, that it is a desirable thing to open a market for inland produce.

Canada is the land of hope; here everything is new; everything going forward; it is scarcely possible for arts, sciences, agriculture, manufactures, to retrograde; they must keep advancing; though in some situations the progress may seem slow, in others they are proportionately rapid.

There is a constant excitement on the minds of emigrants, particularly in the partially settled townships, that greatly assists in keeping them from desponding. The arrival of some enterprising person gives a stimulus to those about him: a profitable speculation is started, and lo, the value of the land in the vicinity rises to double and treble what it was thought worth before; so that, without any design of befriending his neighbours, the schemes of one settler being carried into effect shall benefit a great number. We have already felt the beneficial effect of the access of respectable emigrants locating themselves in this township, as it has already increased the value of our own land in a three-fold degree.

All this, my dear friend, you will say is very well, and might afford subject for a wise discussion between grave men, but will hardly amuse us women; so pray turn to some other theme, and just tell me how you contrive to pass your time among the bears and wolves of Canada.

One lovely day last June I went by water to visit the bridge of a young naval officer, who had purchased a very pretty lot of land some two miles higher up the lake; our party consisted of my husband, baby, and myself; we met a few pleasant friends, and enjoyed our excursion much. Dinner was laid out in the *stoup*, which, as you may not know what is meant by the word, I must tell you that it means a sort of wide verandah, supported by pillars, often of unbarked logs; the floor is either of earth beaten hard, or plank; the roof covered with sheets of bark or else shingled. These stoups are of Dutch origin, and were introduced, I have been told, by the first Dutch settlers in the states, since which they have found their way all over the colonies.

Wreathed with the scarlet creeper, a native plant of our woods and wilds, the wild vine, and also with the hop, which here grows luxuriantly, with no labour or attention to its culture, these stoups have a very rural appearance; in summer serving the purpose of an open ante-room, in which you can take your meals and enjoy the fanning breeze without being inconvenienced by the extreme heat of the noon-day sun.

The situation of the house was remarkably well chosen, just on the summit of a little elevated plain, the ground sloping with a steep descent to a little valley, at the bottom of which a bright rill of water divided the garden from the opposite corn-fields, which clothed a corresponding bank. In front of the stoup, where we dined, the garden was laid out with a smooth plot of grass, surrounded with borders of flowers, and separated from a ripening field of wheat by a light railed fence, over which the luxuriant hop-vine flung its tendrils and graceful blossoms. Now I must tell you the hop is cultivated for the purpose of making a barm for raising bread As you take great interest in housewifery concerns, I shall send you a recipe for what we call hop-rising.

The Yankees use a fermentation of salt, flour, and warm

water or milk; but though the *salt-rising* makes beautiful bread to look at, being far whiter and firmer than the hop-yeast bread, there is a peculiar flavour imparted to the flour that does not please everyone's taste, and it is very difficult to get your salt-rising to work in very cold weather.

And now, having digressed while I gave you my recipes, I shall step back to my party within the stoup, which, I can assure you, was very pleasant, and most cordially disposed to enjoy the meeting. We had books and drawings, and good store of pretty Indian toys, the collection of many long voyages to distant shores, to look at and admire. Soon after sunset we walked down through the woods to the landing at the lake shore, where we found our bark canoe ready to convey us home.

During our voyage, just at the head of the rapids, our attention was drawn to some small object in the water, moving very swiftly along; there were various opinions as to the swimmer, some thinking it to be a water-snake, others a squirrel, or a muskrat; a few swift strokes of the paddles brought us up so to intercept the passage of the little voyager; it proved to be a fine red squirrel, bound on a voyage of discovery from a neighbouring island. The little animal, with a courage and address that astonished his pursuers, instead of seeking safety in a different direction, sprang lightly on the point of the uplifted paddle, and from thence with a bound to the head of my astonished baby, and having gained my shoulder, leaped again into the water, and made direct for the shore, never having deviated a single point from the line he was swimming in when he first came in sight of our canoe. I was surprised and amused by the agility and courage displayed by this innocent creature; I could hardly have given credence to the circumstance had I not been an eye-witness of its conduct, and moreover been wetted plentifully on my shoulder by the sprinkling of water from his coat.

Perhaps you may think my squirrel anecdote incredible; but I can vouch for the truth of it on my own personal experience, as I not only saw but also felt it: the black squirrels are most lovely and elegant animals, considerably larger than the red, the grey, and the striped: the latter are called by the Indians "chit-munks."

We were robbed greatly by these little depredators last sum-

THE BACKWOODS OF CANADA

Catharine Parr Traill

*

The Backwoods of Canada

*

*

*

Selections

Introduction: Clara Thomas

General Editor: Malcolm Ross

New Canadian Library No. 51

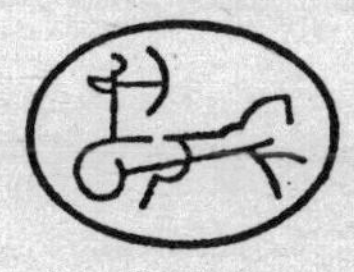

MCCLELLAND & STEWART LIMITED

© in
Canada by
McClelland and Stewart
Limited 1966

Introduction © McClelland
and Stewart Limited 1971

0-7710-9151-6

All rights reserved.
No part of this book may be reproduced in any form without permission in writing from the publishers, except by a reviewer who may quote brief passages in a review to be printed in a magazine or newspaper.

The Canadian Publishers
McClelland and Stewart
Limited
25 Hollinger Road,
Toronto

Printed and bound
in Canada

CONTENTS

*

INTRODUCTION

The publication of this selected edition of Catharine Parr Traill's *The Backwoods of Canada* in the New Canadian Library series completes a significant trilogy of feminine report on Canada in the nineteenth century. Mrs Moodie's *Roughing It in the Bush*, Mrs Jameson's *Winter Studies and Summer Rambles in Canada* and Mrs Traill's *Backwoods* together reveal a comprehensive composite picture taken from three widely ranging angles of vision.

In Mrs Traill's writing, sturdy adaptability to the emigrant's condition, acceptance of the present, and optimism for the future dominate:

> Canada is the land of hope; here everything is new; everything going forward; it is scarcely possible for arts, sciences, agriculture, manufactures to retrograde; they must keep advancing; though in some situations the progress may seem slow, in others they are proportionably rapid.

The style of her writing is unfailingly simple, clear, and factual; its matter-of-factness and lack of dramatic embellishment make *The Backwoods in Canada* an admirable monument to the purpose which Mrs Traill stated in her introduction:

> She prefers honestly representing facts in their real and true light, that the female part of the emigrant's family may be enabled to look them firmly in the face; to find a remedy in female ingenuity and expediency for some difficulties; and, by being properly prepared, encounter the rest with that high-spirited cheerfulness of which women under circumstances the most discouraging, often give extraordinary proofs.

Mrs Traill's book was designed as a handbook for emigrating gentlewomen; its authoress was well-suited, by nature and by training, to produce such a work. She was born in London, England, in 1802, the youngest of nine children of Thomas Strickland, a gentleman of means who moved his family in 1808 to Reydon Hall in Sussex and who took pleasure in encouraging and in superintending the education of his children. The vignettes of Strickland family living which have filtered through time are attractive and familiar ones—an articulate, literary, scribbling family, encouraged by their parents and by the resources of a sizable library to burrow after knowledge and to record their findings. Burneys, Austens, Martineaus, Mills, Murphys (Anna Jameson), Brontës (though sadly blighted)—across time all of these families reveal a similar pattern of indefatigable industry and enthusiasm for stretching minds, imaginations, and writing skills.

At least seven of the Strickland children became published authors: Elizabeth and Agnes were best known for their *Lives of the Queens of England*; Sara and Jane were devoted to far-flung historical horizons, the latter author of *Rome, Regal and Republican*; Susanna's *Roughing It in the Bush* is the best known of a very large literary output; Samuel, after firmly establishing himself in Upper Canada, wrote his account of pioneering, *Twenty-seven Years in Canada West.* Catharine, though the youngest, had been published first: she was the author of nine children's books before she came to Canada.

In 1832 she married Thomas Traill, a retired officer of the Royal Scottish Fusiliers. Immediately they set sail for Canada to take up the grant of land to which Mr Traill was entitled, their destination the Otonabee district of Upper Canada, near the present city of Peterborough. There Samuel Strickland had immigrated some years earlier and shortly afterward the Strickland family Odyssey was completed by the immigration to the same area of Susanna and her husband, Mr Moodie.

The letters which make up *The Backwoods of Canada*, except for four addressed to friends, were written by Catharine Traill to her mother from 1832 to 1835. They were published by Charles Knight in 1836 in his "Library of Entertaining Knowledge," Mrs Traill's introduction designating her particular audience as "the wives and daughters of emigrants of the higher class," her appendices a compendium of factual data ranging from instructions for the making of maple sugar to almanac information regarding numbers and dispersal of immigrants to the Canadas in the years 1829 to 1834. The letters themselves bear strong, if negative, evidence of editing: no extraneous family chit-chat, above all no emotional imbalance, disturb their calm and lucid gentility.

The record begins with the emigrants' departure from

Greenock in July of 1832; it provides a detailed account of their voyage, of their introduction to Canada—and to the cholera, and of their journey to the "interior" where they stayed with brother Samuel near Peterborough until October, when a log-house was ready on their own land. Thereafter the story is one of challenges met and overcome, with a precision of detail provided for others who will follow to find similar conditions, and a substantial assurance of qualified success for those whose hopes are based on reality, industry, and what Mrs Traill would call "sound domestic economy."

Every line evidences the maturity and commonsense of the author; such a book might have been written by Elizabeth Bennet if, already tempered in Jane Austen's furnace, she and Mr Darcy had deemed emigration necessary for the future of their family fortunes. Catharine Traill was sustained by firmer and far more positive considerations than a naïve optimism would provide. She had a healthy respect for property and a strong sense of family position and solidarity:

> Children should be taught to appreciate the devoted love that has induced their parents to overcome the natural reluctance felt by all persons to quit forever the land of their forefathers . . . that their children may be placed in a situation in which, by industry and activity, the substantial comforts of life may be permanently obtained, and a landed property handed down to them and their children after them.

She walked easily with the conventions of her class and time—allegiance to the Crown and its representatives, a distrust of all things "republican" and American. Her most emotional prose, though still conventionally rhetorical, denounces the Mackenzie rebellion in letters written later than the *Backwoods* collection:

> Mackenzie raised the cry of rebellion, and the answer has been the rallying of thousands and tens of thousands of valiant men round the standard of their young Queen—with the thrilling cry echoed from lake to lake and forest to plains "Long live Victoria and the British Constitution."

Conventional pieties do not impinge upon the reader, but the impression of religious faith is strong, as is the impression of an independent spirit recording with knowledgeable appreciation the advantages which accrue to her new position:

> I was too much inclined to spurn with impatience the fetters that etiquette and fashion are wont to impose on society till they rob its followers of all freedom and independence of will. . . . And I must freely confess to you that I do prize and enjoy my present liberty in this country exceedingly: in this we possess the advantage over you.

Catharine Traill found in Canadian nature the sustaining and compensating substitute for all those niceties of polite civilization for which many emigrant women mourned hopelessly. She had the priceless sense of wonder at both the magnificence and the precision of nature which has been the most excellently communicated quality of Canada's artists and poets. Sometimes she described the grandeur of a scene with an apt, but conventionally romantic, technique:

> I have stood of a bright winter day looking with infinite delight on the beautiful mimic waterfalls congealed into solid ice along the bank of the river; and by the mill-dam, from contemplating these pretty frolics of Father Frost, I have been led to picture to myself the sublime scenery of the Arctic regions.

Always, however, the individual and the precise in nature called forth all the curiosity and delicacy of observation, the skill and elegance of description of the knowledgeable botanist. Catharine Traill had been an enthusiastic amateur in botany since girlhood; in Canada she found unlimited scope for her interests and for her self-training. Her *Canadian Wild Flowers* (1868) and *Studies in Plant Life in Canada* (1885) are classic records of nineteenth-century Canadian flora and the climactic works of her writing career; they brought her fame as a distinguished naturalist, an encouraging gift of £100 from the British government, and in 1893 an island in the river Otonabee, an acknowledgement of her work by the Canadian government.

The Backwoods of Canada gives early and ample evidence of Mrs Traill's propensity. In two paragraphs she disposes of her attack of cholera, the most dreaded epidemic of the 30's and a plague that killed thousands of immigrants; some eighteen pages are required, however, to record with the precision of the scientist and the fresh delight of the discoverer the wild-flowers she finds around her new home:

> I have promised to collect some of the most singular of our native flowers for one of the Professors of Botany in the Edinburgh University. . . . A very beautiful plant of the lily tribe abounds both in our woods and clearings . . . the flower is either deep red, or of a dazzling white, though the latter is often found stained with a delicate blush-pink, or a deep green; the latter appears to be caused by the calix running into the petal . . . the flower consists of three petals, the calix three; it belongs to the class and order *Hexandria monogynia*; style, three-cleft; seed-vessel of three valves.

Something of the same precise expression of observation is evident in her descriptions of the Indians living in the Peterborough district. To them she brought a warm curiosity and the acceptance of a way of life utterly alien to her, but one which she depicted with a keen eye for its colour, a full realization of its transience, and notably without emotional case-making. This section of *The Backwoods of Canada* was part of a lengthy excerpt used by Mr N. P. Willis in the text of *Canadian Scenery*, the *de luxe* publication of 1842, illustrated by the many drawings of W. H. Bartlett.

Catharine Parr Traill wrote seventeen books, eight of them after coming to Canada, and, in addition, many occasional pieces —she was, for example, a frequent contributor to John Lovell's Montreal publication, *The Literary Garland*. She and her husband had a family of nine children, a conspicuous contribution of the kind of settler nineteenth-century Canada most needed. She died in her ninety-eighth year, her naturalist's interest alert to the very end of her life.

Her most popular book for children was called, fittingly, *Canadian Crusoes* (1853). There was much of Crusoe in Catharine Traill: her mind was rational, empiric, and scientific in its bent and her writing talents were best employed when she recorded her observing and experiencing of her new environment. *The Backwoods of Canada* provides none of the histrionics which are so much a part of the writing of Susanna Moodie or of Anna Jameson; it gives us instead a portrait and a record of the woman Catharine Parr Traill was and wished to be—a pioneer gentlewoman, superbly equipped for her rôle, eminently successful in it, and notably fitted for the advising of others who would follow in her path.

CLARA THOMAS

York University,
Toronto,
February, 1965.

CHAPTER 1 *The Ocean Voyage*

Brig *Laurel*, July 18, 1832.

I received your last kind letter, my dearest mother, only a few hours before we set sail from Greenock. As you express a wish that I should give you a minute detail of our voyage, I shall take up my subject from the time of our embarkation, and write as inclination prompts me. Instead of having reason to complain of short letters, you will, I fear, find mine only too prolix.

After many delays and disappointments, we succeeded at last in obtaining a passage in a fast-sailing brig, the *Laurel*, of Greenock; and favourable winds are now rapidly carrying us across the Atlantic.

The *Laurel* is not a regular passenger-ship, which I consider an advantage, for what we lose in amusement and variety we assuredly gain in comfort. The cabin is neatly fitted up, and I enjoy the luxury (for such it is, compared with the narrow berths of the state cabin) of a handsome sofa, with crimson draperies, in the great cabin. The state cabin is also ours. We paid fifteen pounds each for our passage to Montreal. This was high, but it includes every expense; and, in fact, we had no choice. The only vessel in the river bound for Canada was a passenger-ship, literally swarming with emigrants, chiefly of the lower class of Highlanders.

The only passengers besides ourselves in the *Laurel* are the captain's nephew, a pretty yellow-haired lad, about fifteen years of age, who works his passage out, and a young gentleman who is going out as clerk in a merchant's house in Quebec. He seems too much wrapped up in his own affairs to be very communicative to others.

I was much pleased with the scenery of the Clyde; the day we set sail was a lovely one, and I remained on deck till nightfall. The morning light found our vessel dashing gallantly along, with a favourable breeze, through the North Channel; that day we saw the last of the Hebrides, and before night lost sight of the north coast of Ireland. A wide expanse of water and sky is now our only prospect, unvaried by any object save the distant and scarcely to be traced outline of some vessel just seen at the verge of the horizon, a speck in the immensity of space, or sometimes a few sea-fowl. I love to watch these wanderers of the ocean as they rise and fall with the rocking billows or flit about our vessel; and often I wonder whence they came, to what distant shore they are bound, and if they make the rude wave their home and resting-place during the long day and dark night; and then I recall to mind the words of the American poet, Bryant,

> He who from zone to zone
> Guides through the boundless air their certain flight,
> In the long way that I must tread alone
> Will guide my steps aright.

Though we have been little more than a week on board, I am getting weary of the voyage. I can only compare the monotony of it to being weather-bound in some country inn. I have already made myself acquainted with all the books worth reading in the ship's library; unfortunately, it is chiefly made up with old novels and musty romances.

I have endured the horrors of *mal de mer*, and except when the weather is fine I sit on a bench on the deck, wrapped in my cloak, and sew, or pace the deck with my husband, and talk over plans for the future, which in all probability will never be realized. I really do pity men who are not actively employed: women have always their needle as a resource against the overwhelming weariness of an idle life; but where a man is confined to a small space, such as the deck and cabin of a trading vessel, with nothing to see, nothing to hear, nothing to do, and nothing to read, he is really a very pitiable creature. Every space is utilized in a ship. The bench on which the bed of cloaks is spread for me covers the hen coop. Poor prisoners to be killed and cooked as needed!

There is one passenger on board that seems perfectly happy, if one may judge from the liveliness of the songs with which he greets us whenever we approach his cage. It is "Harry," the captain's goldfinch—"the *captain's mate*," as the sailors term him. This pretty creature has made no fewer than twelve voyages in the *Laurel*. "It is all one to him whether his cage is at sea or on land, he is still at home," said the captain, regarding his little favourite with an air of great affection.

I have already formed a friendship with the little captive. He never fails to greet my approach with one of his sweetest songs, and will take from my fingers a bit of biscuit, which he holds in his claws till he has thanked me with a few of his clearest notes. This mark of acknowledgement is termed by the steward, "saying grace." But his master views my attentions to his beloved "Harry" with a jealous eye. He has neither wife nor child to love him; he says, "I cannot afford to lose the least bit of Harry's love. I want it all."

The bird has no mate. It made twelve voyages to and fro to the West Indies with him.

If the wind still continues to favour us, the captain tells us we shall be on the banks of Newfoundland in another week. Farewell for the present.

CHAPTER 2 *Majestic and Mighty River*

Brig *Laurel*, River St Laurence,
August 6, 1832.

... We came within sight of the shores of Newfoundland on the 5th of August, just one month from the day we took our last look of the British Isles. Yet though the coast was brown, and rugged, and desolate, I hailed its appearance with rapture. Never did anything seem so refreshing and delicious to me as the land breeze that came to us bearing health and gladness on its wings. I had become very weak but soon revived as I felt the air from the land reaching us and some winged insects came to us—a welcome sight.

I had noticed with some curiosity the restless activity of the captain's bird some hours previous to "land" being proclaimed from the look-out station. He sang continually, and his note was longer, clearer, and more thrilling than heretofore; the little creature, the captain assured me, was conscious of the difference in the air as we approached the land. "I trust almost as much to my bird as to my glass," he said.

Our progress was somewhat tedious after we entered the gulf.

Ninety miles across is the entrance of this majestic river; it seems an ocean in itself. Half our time is spent poring over the great chart in the cabin, which is constantly being rolled and unrolled by my husband to gratify my desire of learning the names of the distant shores and islands which we pass.

We are without a pilot yet, and the captain being a cautious seaman is unwilling to risk the vessel on this dangerous navigation; so that we proceed but slowly on our voyage.

August 7—We were visited this morning by a beautiful little bird, not much larger than our gold-crested wren. I hailed it as a bird of good omen—a little messenger sent to bid us welcome to the New World, and I felt almost a childish joy at the sight of our little visitor. There are happy moments in our lives when we draw the greatest pleasure from the most trifling sources, as children are pleased with the most simple toy.

From the hour we entered the gulf a perceptible change had taken place in all on board. The captain, a man of grave, quiet manners, grew quite talkative. My husband was more than usually animated, and even the thoughtful young Scotchman became positively an entertaining person. The crew displayed the most lively zeal in the performance of their duty, and the goldfinch sang cheerily from dawn till sunset. As for me, hope was busy in my heart, chasing from it all feelings of doubt or regret that might sadden the present or cloud the future.

I am now able to trace distinctly the outline of the coast on the southern side of the river. Sometimes the high lands are suddenly enveloped in dense clouds of mist, which are in constant motion, rolling along in shadowy billows, now tinted with rosy light, now white and fleecy, or bright as silver, as they catch the sunbeams. So rapid are the changes that take place on this fog-bank that perhaps the next time I raise my eyes I behold the scene changed as if by magic. The misty curtain is slowly drawn up, as if by invisible hands, and the wild, wooded mountains partially revealed, with their bold, rocky shores and sweeping bays. At other times the vapoury volume, dividing, moves along the valleys and deep ravines like lofty pillars of smoke, or hangs in snowy draperies among the dark forest pines.

I am never weary of watching these fantastic clouds; they recall to me the pleasant time I spent in the Highlands among the cloud-capped hills of the north.

As yet, the air is cold, and we experience frequent squalls of wind and hail, with occasional peals of thunder; then again all is serene and bright, and the air is filled with fragrance, and flies and bees and birds come flitting past us from the shore.

August 8—Though I cannot but dwell with feelings of wonder and admiration on the majesty and power of this mighty river, I begin to grow weary of its immensity, and long for a nearer view of the shore; but at present we see nothing more than long lines of pine-clad hills, with here and there white specks, which they tell me are settlements and villages to the south; while huge mountains divested of verdure bound our view on the north side of the river. My admiration of mountainous scenery makes me dwell with more interest on that side of the river, and I watch the progress of cultivation among these rugged and inhospitable regions with positive pleasure.

During the last two days we have been anxiously looking out for a pilot to take us up to Quebec. Various signals have been fired, but hitherto without success; no pilot has condescended to visit us, so we are somewhat in the condition of a stage without a coachman, with only some inexperienced hand to hold the reins. I already perceive some manifestations of impatience appearing among us, but no one blames the captain, who is very anxious about the matter, as the river is full of rocks and shoals, and presents many difficulties to a person not intimately acquainted with the navigation. Besides, he is answerable for the safety of the ship to the underwriters in case he neglects to take a pilot on board.

* * *

While writing the above I was roused by a bustle on deck, and going up to learn the cause was informed that a boat with the long looked-for pilot had put off from the shore; but, after all the fuss and bustle, it proved only a French fisherman, with a poor ragged lad, his assistant. The captain with very little difficulty persuaded Monsieur Paul Breton to pilot us as far as Green Island, a distance of some hundred miles higher up the river, where he assured us we should meet with a regular pilot, if not before.

I have some little difficulty in understanding Monsieur Paul, as he speaks a peculiar patois; but he seems good-natured and obliging enough. He tells us the wheat is yet green, hardly in ear, and the summer fruits not yet ripe; but he says that at Quebec we shall find apples and fruit in plenty.

As we advance higher up the river, the country on both sides begins to assume a more genial aspect. Patches of verdure, with white cottages, are seen on the shores and scattered along the sides of the mountains; while here and there a village church rears its simple spire, distinguished above the surrounding buildings by its glittering vane and bright roof of tin. The southern shores are more populous but less picturesque than those of the north, but there is enough on either side to delight the eye.

This morning we anchored off the Isle of Bic, a pretty, low island, covered with trees and looking very pleasant. I felt a longing desire to set my foot on Canadian ground, and must own I was a little disappointed when the captain advised me to remain on board, and not attempt to make one of the party that were preparing to go on shore: my husband seconded the captain's wish, so I contented myself with leaning over the ship's side and feasting my eyes on the rich masses of foliage as they waved to and fro with the slight breeze that agitated them. I soon had reason to be thankful that I had not followed my own wayward will, for the afternoon proved foggy, and on the return of the boat I learned that the ground was swampy just where the party landed, and that they sank over their ankles in water. They reported the island to be covered knee-deep with a most luxuriant growth of white clover, tall trees, low shrubs, and an abundance of wild flowers.

That I might not regret not accompanying him, my husband brought me a delightful bouquet which he had selected for me. Among the flowers were fragrant red roses, *rosa lucida*, resembling those we call Scotch burnt-leaved, with smooth shining leaves and few if any thorns; the blue flower, Pulmonaria or Lungwort, which I had gathered in the Highlands; a pea with red blossoms and wreaths of lovely pale green foliage; a white fringed orchis, the smell of which was quite delicious. Besides these were several small white and yellow loosestrife flowers, and others with which I was totally unacquainted. The steward furnished me with a china jar and fresh water, so that I shall have the pleasure of a bouquet during the rest of the voyage. The sailors had not forgotten a green bough or two to adorn the ship, and the bird-cage was soon as bowery as leaves could make it. . . .

The Backwoods of Canada

August 16—We reached Grosse Isle yesterday evening. It is a beautiful rocky island, covered with groves of beech, birch, ash, and fir trees. There are several vessels lying at anchor close to the shore; one bears the melancholy symbol of disease, the yellow flag; she is a passenger-ship, and has the smallpox and measles among her crew. When any infectious complaint appears on board, the yellow flag is hoisted, and the invalids conveyed to the cholera-hospital, a wooden building that had been erected on a rising bank above the shore. It is surrounded with palisadoes and a guard of soldiers.

There is also a temporary fort at some distance from the hospital, containing a garrison of soldiers, who are there to enforce the quarantine rules. These rules are considered as very defective, and in some respects quite absurd, and are productive of many severe evils to the unfortunate emigrants.

When the passengers and crew of a vessel do not exceed a certain number, they are not allowed to land, under a penalty both to the captain and to the offender; but if, on the contrary, they should exceed the stated number, *ill* or *well*, passengers and crew must all turn out and go on shore, taking with them their bedding and clothes, which are all spread out on the shore, to be washed, aired, and fumigated, giving the healthy every chance of taking the infection from the invalids near them. The sheds and buildings put up for the accommodation of those who are obliged to submit to the quarantine laws are in the same area as the hospital.

Nothing can exceed the longing desire I feel to be allowed to land and explore this picturesque island; the weather is so fine and the waving groves so green; the little rocky bays and inlets of the island appear so tempting; but to all my entreaties the visiting surgeon who came on board returned a decided negative.

A few hours after his visit, however, an Indian basket, containing strawberries and raspberries, with a large bunch of wild flowers, was sent on board for me with the surgeon's compliments.

I amuse myself with making little sketches of the surrounding scenery, or watching the groups of emigrants on shore. We have already seen the landing of the passengers of three emigrant ships. You may imagine yourself looking on a fair or crowded market, clothes waving in the wind or spread out on the earth, chests, bundles, baskets, men, women, and children, asleep or basking in the sun, some in motion busied with their goods, the women employed in washing or cooking in the open air beside the wood fires on the beach; while parties of children are pursuing each other in wanton glee, rejoicing in their newly-acquired liberty. Mixed with these you see the stately form and gay trappings of the sentinels, while the thin blue smoke of the wood fires, rising above the trees, heightens the picture and gives it an additional effect. On my husband remarking the picturesque appearance of the scene before us to one of the officers from the fort who had come on board, he smiled sadly, and replied, "Believe me, in this instance, as in many others, 'tis distance lends enchantment to the view. Could you take a nearer survey of some of those very picturesque groups which you admire, I think you would turn away from them with heart-sickness; you would there behold every variety of disease, vice, poverty, filth, and famine—human misery in its most disgusting and saddening forms; such pictures as Hogarth's pencil only could have portrayed, or Crabbe's pen described."

I petitioned the health officer's permission to go on shore at a wild spot far from the quarantine ground, but he was inexorable. I pleaded: "There is no one there; it will do no harm." "You think so, Madam, but you might see a redcoat with a bayonet among those green bushes to warn you off," he said with a grim smile. I was silenced.

August 17— . . . At ten last night, August the 16th, the lights of the city of Quebec were seen gleaming through the distance like a coronet of stars above the waters. At half-past ten we dropped anchor opposite the fort, and I fell asleep dreaming of the various scenes through which I had passed. Again I was destined to be disappointed in my expectations of going on shore. Pity my disappointment! The captain promised us a treat of new milk, white bread, and fruit. Alas! it was not to be. The words came to my mind, and only too true they proved:

The best laid schemes of mice and men
Gang aft agley.

Our fine play was never acted out. The visiting surgeon advised my husband by no means to land, as the mortality that still raged in the town made it very hazardous. He gave a melancholy description of the place. "Desolation and woe and great mourning—Rachel weeping for her children because they are not," are words that may well be applied to this city of the pestilence.

Nothing can be more imposing than the situation of Quebec, built on the sides and summit of a magnificent rock, on the highest point of which (Cape Diamond) stands the fortress overlooking the river, and commanding a most superb view of the surrounding scenes. I did, indeed, regret the loss of this noble prospect, the equal of which I suppose I shall never see. It would have been something to have thought on and recalled in after years, when buried in the solitude of the Canadian woods.

The opposite heights, being the Point Levis side, are highly picturesque, though less imposing than the rock on which the town stands. The bank is rocky, precipitous, and clothed with trees that sweep down to the water's edge, excepting where they are cleared away to give place to white cottages, gardens, and hanging orchards. But, in my opinion, much less is done with this romantic situation than might be effected if good taste were exercised in the buildings, and on the disposal of the ground. How lovely would such a spot be rendered in England or Scotland! Nature here has done all, and man but little, excepting sticking up some ugly wooden cottages, as mean as they are tasteless. It is, however, very possible there may be pretty villas and houses higher up, that are concealed from the eye by the intervening groves.

The river is considered to be just a mile across from Point Levis to the landing-stairs below the custom-house in Quebec; and it was a source of amusement to me to watch the horse ferry-boats that ply between the two shores. The captain told me there were not less than twelve of these comical-looking machines. They each have their regular hours, so that you see a constant succession going or returning. They carry a strange assortment of passengers: well- and ill-dressed; old and young; rich and poor; cows, sheep, horses, pigs, dogs, fowls, market-baskets, vegetables, fruit, hay, corn, anything and everything you will see by turns.

The boat is flat, railed round, with a wicket at each end to admit the live and dead stock that go out or are taken on board; the centre of the boat (if such it can be called) is occupied by four lean, ill-favoured hacks, who walk round and round, as if in a threshing machine, and work the paddles at each side. There is a sort of pen for the cattle.

I am told there is a monument erecting in honour of Wolfe, in the Governor's garden, looking towards the St Laurence, and to be seen from Point Levis; the inscription has not yet been decided upon.

The captain has just returned from the town. He very kindly brought on board a basket of ripe apples for me, besides fresh meat, vegetables, bread, butter, and milk. The deck is all bustle with custom-house officers, and men unloading a part of the ship's freight, which consists chiefly of rum, brandy, sugar, and coals, for ballast. We are to leave Quebec by five o'clock this evening. The *British America*, a superb steam-vessel of three decks, takes us in tow as far an Montreal. I must now say farewell.

CHAPTER 3 *Up River to Montreal*

Brig *Laurel*, St Laurence, below Montreal,
August 17, 1832.

. . . I was anxious to obtain a near view of a log-house or a shanty, and was somewhat disappointed in the few buildings of this kind that I saw along the banks of the river. It was not the rudeness of the material so much as the barn-like form of the buildings of this kind, and the little attention that was paid to the picturesque, that displeased me. In Britain even the peasant has a taste enough to plant a few roses or honeysuckles about his door or his casement, and there is the little bit of garden enclosed and neatly kept; but here no such attempt is made to ornament the cottages. We saw no smiling orchard or grove to conceal the bare log walls; and as to the little farm-houses, they are uglier still, and look so pert and ungraceful stuck upon the bank close to the water's edge.

Farther back a different style of building and cultivation appears. The farms and frame-houses are really handsome places, and in good taste, with clumps of trees here and there to break the monotony of the clearing. The land is nearly one unbroken level plain, apparently fertile and well farmed, but too flat for fine scenery. To my unpractised eye the dead level extent of country gave me the idea that all that wide space of land had once been a vast lake, and the few elevated spots islands on the surface. The country between Quebec and Montreal has all the appearance of having been under a long state of cultivation, especially on the right bank of the river. Still there is a great portion of forest standing which it will take years of labour to remove.

We passed some little grassy islands on which there were many herds of cattle feeding. I was puzzling myself to know how they got there, when the captain told me it was usual for farmers to convey their stock to these island pastures in flat-bottomed boats, or to swim them, if the place was fordable, and leave them to graze as long as the food continued good. If cows are put on an island within a reasonable distance of the farm, some person goes daily in a canoe to milk them. While he was telling me this, a log-canoe with a boy and a stout lass with tin pails paddled across from the bank of the river and proceeded to call together their herd.

We noticed some very pleasant rural villages to the right as we advanced, but our pilot was stupid, and could not, or would not, tell their names. It was Sunday morning, and we could just hear the quick tinkling of the church bells, and distinguish long lines of calèches, light waggons, with equestrians and pedestrians hastening along the avenue of trees that led to the churchyard; besides these, were boats and canoes crossing the river, bound to the same peaceful haven.

In a part of the St Laurence, where the channel is rendered difficult by shoals and sand-banks, there occur little lighthouses, looking somewhat like miniature watermills, on wooden posts, raised above the flat banks on which they are built. These droll little huts were inhabited, and we noticed a merry party, in their holiday clothes, enjoying a gossip with a party in a canoe below them. They looked clean and smart, and cheerful enough, but I did not envy them their situation, which I should think far from healthy.

Some miles below Montreal the appearance of the country became richer, more civilized, and populous; while the distant line of blue mountains, at the verge of the horizon, added an interest to the landscape. The rich tint of ripened harvest formed a beautiful contrast with the azure sky and waters of the St Laurence. The scenery of the river near Montreal is of a very different character to that below Quebec; the latter possesses a wild and rugged aspect, and its productions are evidently those of a colder and less happy climate. What the former loses in grandeur and picturesque effect, it gains in fertility of soil and warmth of temperature. In the lower division of the Province you feel that the industry of the inhabitants is forcing a churlish soil for bread; while in the upper, the land seems willing to yield her increase to a moderate exertion. Remember, these are merely the cursory remarks of a passing traveller, and founded on no personal experience.

There was a feeling of anxiety and dread upon our minds that we would hardly acknowledge to each other as we drew near to the city of the pestilence, as if ashamed of confessing a weakness that was felt; but no one spoke on the subject. With what unmixed delight and admiration at any other time should we have gazed on the scene that opened upon us.

The river here expands into a fine extensive lakelike basin, diversified with islands, on the largest of which Montreal is situated.

The lofty hill from which the town takes its name rises like a crown above it, and forms a singular and magnificent feature in the landscape, reminding me of some of the detached hills in the vicinity of Inverness.

Opposite to the Quebec suburbs [sic], just in front of the rapids, is situated the island of St Helen's, a spot of infinite loveliness. The centre of it is occupied by a grove of lofty trees, while the banks, sloping down to the water, seem of the most verdant turf. The scene was heightened by the appearance of the troops which garrison the island. The white tents and gay scarlet coats of the soldiers enlivened the scene.

The shores of the river, studded with richly cultivated farms; the village of Laprairie, with the little island of St Anne's in the distance; the glittering steeples and roofs of the city, with its gardens and villas, looked lovely by the softened glow of a Canadian summer sunset.

The church bells ringing for evening prayer, with the hum of voices from the shore, mingled not inharmoniously with the rush of the rapids.

These rapids are caused by a descent in the bed of the river. In some places this declination is gradual, in others sudden and abrupt. Where the current is broken by masses of limestone or granite rock, as at the Cascades, the Cedars, and the Long Sault, it creates whirlpools and cataracts. But the rapids below Montreal are not of this magnificent character, being made perceptible only by the unusual swiftness of the water, and its surface being disturbed by foam and waving lines and dimples. In short, I was disappointed in my expectation of seeing something very grand, and was half angry at these prettily behaved quiet rapids, to the foot of which we were towed in good style by our faithful consort the *British America*.

As the captain is uncertain how long he may be detained at Montreal, I shall send this letter without further delay, and write again as soon as possible.

CHAPTER 4 *Impressions of City and Country*

Nelson Hotel, Montreal, August 21.

. . . I was greatly disappointed in my first acquaintance with the interior of Montreal; a place of which travellers had said so much. I could compare it only to the fruits of the Dead Sea, which are said to be fair and tempting to look upon, but yield only ashes and bitterness when tasted by the thirsty traveller.

I noticed one peculiar feature in the buildings along the suburb facing the river—that they were mostly furnished with broad wooden balconies from the lower to the upper story; in some instances they surrounded the houses on three sides, and seemed to form a sort of outer chamber. Some of these balconies were ascended by flights of broad stairs from the outside.

I remember, when a child, dreaming of houses so constructed, and fancying them very delightful; and so I think they might be rendered, if shaded by climbing shrubs and adorned with flowers, to represent a hanging-garden or sweet-scented bowery walk. But nothing of this kind gladdened our eyes as we toiled along the hot streets. Every house of public resort was crowded from the top to the bottom with emigrants of all ages, English, Irish, and Scotch. The sounds of riotous merriment that burst from them seemed but ill assorted with the haggard, care-worn faces of many of the thoughtless revellers.

The contrast was only too apparent and too painful a subject to those that looked upon this show of outward gaiety and inward misery.

The cholera had made awful ravages, and its devastating effects were to be seen in the darkened dwellings and the mourning habiliments of all classes. An expression of dejection and anxiety appeared in the faces of the few persons we encountered in our walk to the hotel, which plainly indicated the state of their minds.

In some situations whole streets had been nearly depopulated; those that were able fled panic-stricken to the country villages, while others remained to die in the bosom of their families.

To no class, I am told, has the disease proved so fatal as to the poorer sort of emigrants. Many of these, debilitated by the privations and fatigue of a long voyage, on reaching Quebec or Montreal indulged in every sort of excess, especially the dangerous one of intoxication; and, as if purposely paving the way to certain destruction, they fell immediate victims to the complaint.

In one house eleven persons died, in aother seventeen; a little child of seven years old was the only creature left to tell the woeful tale. This poor desolate orphan was taken by the nuns to their benevolent institution, where every attention was paid that humanity could suggest. . . .

The river-side portion of the town is entirely mercantile. Its narrow, dirty streets and dark houses, with heavy iron shutters, have a disagreeable appearance, which cannot but make an unfavourable impression on the mind of a British traveller. The other portion of the town, however, is of a different character, and the houses are interspersed with gardens and pleasant walks, which looked very agreeable from the windows of the ballroom of the Nelson Hotel. This room, which is painted from top to bottom, the walls and ceiling, with a coarse imitation of groves and Canadian scenery, commands a superb view of the city, the river, and all the surrounding country, taking in the distant mountains of Chambly, the shores of the St Laurence, towards Laprairie, and the rapids above and below the island of St Anne's. The royal mountain (Mont Real), with its wooded sides, its rich scenery, and its city with its streets and public buildings, lie at your feet: with such objects before you the eye may well be charmed with the scenery of Montreal.

We receive the greatest attention from the master of the hotel, who is an Italian. The servants of the house are very civil, and the company that we meet are the ordinary very respectable, chiefly emigrants like ourselves, with some lively French men and women. The table is well supplied, and the charges for board and lodging one dollar per day each.

I am amused with the variety of characters of which our table is composed. Some of the emigrants appear to entertain the most sanguine hopes of success, appearing to foresee no difficulties in carrying their schemes into effect. As a contrast to these there is one of my countrymen, just returned from the western district on his way back to England, who entreats us by no means to go farther up this horrid country, as he emphatically styles the Upper Province, assuring us he would not live in it for all the land it contained.

He had been induced, by reading Cattermole's pamphlet on the subject of Emigration, to quit a good farm, and gathering together what property he possessed, to embark for Canada. Encouraged by the advice of a friend in this country, he purchased a lot of wild land in the western district; "but, sir," said he, addressing my husband with much vehemence, "I found I had been vilely deceived. Such land, such a country—I would not live in it for all I could see. Why, there is not a drop of wholesome water to be got, or a potato that is fit to eat. I lived for two months in a miserable shed they call a shanty, eaten up alive with mosquitoes. I could get nothing to eat but salted pork, and, in short, the discomforts are unbearable. And then all my farming knowledge was quite useless—people know nothing about farming in this country. Why, it would have broken my heart to work among the stumps, and never see such a thing as a well-ploughed field. And then," he added, in a softer tone, "I thought of my poor wife and the little one. I might, for the sake of bettering my condition, have roughed out a year or so myself, but, poor thing, I could not have had the heart to have brought her out from the comforts of England to such a place, not so good as one of our cow-houses or stables, and so I shall just go home; and if I don't tell all my neighbours what sort of a country this is they are all crazing to throw up their farms and come to, never trust a word of mine again."

It was to no purpose that some persons present argued with him on the folly of returning until he had tried what could be done: he only told them they were fools if they stayed an hour in a country like this; and ended by execrating those persons who deceived the people at home by their false statements, who sum up in a few pages all the advantages, without filling a volume with the disadvantages, as they might well do. . . .

Cobourg, August 29—When I closed my last letter I told you, my dear mother, that we should leave Montreal by sunrise the following day; but in this we were doomed to be disappointed, and to experience the truth of these words: "Boast not thyself of tomorrow, for thou knowest not what an hour may bring forth." Early that very morning, just an hour before sunrise, I was seized with the symptoms of the fatal malady that had made so many homes desolate. I was too ill to commence my journey, and, with a heavy heart, heard the lumbering wheels of the stage that we had taken our places in for Lachine rattle over the stones from the door of the hotel.

I hourly grew worse, till the sister of the landlady, an excellent young woman, who had previously shown me great attention, persuaded me to send for a physician; and my husband, distracted at seeing me in such agony, ran off to seek for the best medical aid. After some little delay a physician was found. I was then in extreme torture; but was relieved by bleeding, and by the violent fits of sickness that ensued. I will not dwell minutely on my sufferings; suffice to say, they were intense; but God, in His mercy, though He chastened and afflicted me, yet gave me not over unto death. From the females of the house I received the greatest kindness. Instead of fleeing affrighted from the chamber of sickness, the two Irish girls almost quarrelled which should be my attendant; while Jane Taylor, the good young woman I before mentioned, never left me from the time I grew so alarmingly ill till a change for the better had come over me, but, at the peril of her own life, supported me in her arms, and held me on her bosom when I was struggling with mortal agony, alternately speaking peace to me and striving to sooth the anguish of my poor afflicted partner.

The remedies applied were bleeding, a portion of opium, blue pill, and some sort of salts—not the common Epsom. The remedies proved effectual, though I suffered much from sickness and headache for many hours. The debility and low fever that took the place of the cholera, obliged me to keep my bed some days. During the first two my doctor visited me four times a day; he was very kind, and, on hearing that I was the wife of a British officer emigrating to the Upper Province, he seemed more than ever interested in my recovery, evincing a sympathy for us that was very grateful to our feelings. After a weary confinement of several days, I was at last pronounced in a sufficiently convalescent state to begin my journey, though still so weak that I was scarcely able to support myself. . . .

With the exception of Quebec and Montreal, I must give the preference to the Upper Province. If not on so grand a scale, the scenery is more calculated to please, from the appearance of industry and fertility it displays. I am delighted, in travelling along the road, with the neatness, cleanliness, and comfort of the cottages and farms. The log-house and shanty rarely occur, having been supplanted by pretty frame-houses, built in a superior style, and often painted white-lead colour or a pale pea-green. Around these habitations were orchards, bending down with a rich harvest of apples, plums, and the American crab, those beautiful little scarlet apples so often met with as a wet preserve among our sweetmeats at home.

You see none of the signs of poverty or its attendant miseries. No ragged, dirty, squalid children, dabbling in mud or dust; but many a tidy, smart-looking lass was spinning at the cottage-doors, with bright eyes and braided locks, while the younger girls were seated on the green turf or on the threshold, knitting and singing as blithe as birds.

There is something very picturesque in the great spinning-wheels that are used in this country for spinning wool, and if attitude were to be studied among our Canadian lasses, there cannot be one more becoming, or calculated to show off the natural advantages of a fine figure, than spinning at the big wheel. The spinster does not sit, but walks to and fro, guiding the yarn with one hand while with the other she turns the wheel.

I often noticed, as we passed by the cottage farms, hanks of yarn of different colours hanging on the garden or orchard fence to dry; there were all manner of colours, green, blue, purple, brown, red, and white. A civil landlady, at whose tavern we stopped to change horses, told me these hanks of yarn were first spun and then dyed by the good wives, preparatory to being sent to the loom. She showed me some of this home-spun cloth, which really looked very well. It was a dullish dark brown, the wool being the produce of a breed of black sheep. This cloth is made up in different ways for family use. A mixture of white and black wool gives the brown color, or else white dyed with Butternut.

"Every little dwelling you see," said she, "has its lot of land, and, consequently, its flock of sheep; and, as the children are early taught to spin and knit, and help to dye the yarn, their parents can afford to see them well and comfortably clothed.

"Many of these very farms you now see in so thriving a condition were wild land thirty years ago, nothing but Indian hunting-grounds. The industry of men, and many of them poor men, that had not a rood of land of their own in their own country, has effected this change."

I was much gratified by the reflection to which this good woman's information gave rise. "We also are going to purchase wild land, and why may not we see our farm, in process of time," thought I, "equal these fertile spots. Surely this is a blessed country to which we have emigrated," said I, pursuing the pleasing idea, "where every cottage abounds with the comforts and necessaries of life."

I perhaps overlooked at that time the labour, the difficulties, the privations to which these settlers had been exposed when they first came to this country. I saw it only at a distance of many years, under a high state of cultivation, perhaps in the hands of their children or their children's children, while the toil-worn parent's head was low in the dust.

Among other objects my attention was attracted by the appearance of open burying-grounds by the roadside. Pretty green mounds, surrounded by groups of walnut and other handsome timber trees, contained the graves of a family, or may be, some favoured friends slept quietly below the turf beside them. If the ground was not consecrated, it was hallowed by the tears and prayers of parents and children. . . .

After some difficulty in obtaining sight of the landlady of the inn at Cornwall, and asking her to show me a chamber where we might pass the night, with a most ungracious air she pointed to a door which opened into a mere closet, in which was a bed divested of curtains, one chair, and an apology for a wash-stand. Seeing me in some dismay at the sight of this uninviting domicile, she laconically observed there was that or none, unless I chose to sleep in a four-bedded room, which had three tenants in it—and those gentlemen. This alternative I somewhat indignantly declined, and in no very good humour retired to my cabin, where vile familiars to the dormitory kept us from closing our weary eyelids till the break of day.

We took an early and hasty breakfast, and again commenced our journey. Here our party consisted of myself, my husband, a lady and gentleman with three small children, besides an infant of a month old, all of whom, from the eldest to the youngest, were suffering from whooping-cough; two great Cumberland miners, and a French pilot and his companion—this was a huge amphibious-looking monster, who bounced in and squeezed himself into a corner seat, giving a knowing nod and comical grin to the driver, who was in the secret, and who, in utter defiance of all remonstrance at this unlooked-for intrusion, cracked his whip with a flourish that appeared to be reckoned pretty considerably smart by two American travellers that stood on either side the door at the inn, with their hats not in their hands nor yet on their heads, but slung by a black ribbon to one of their waistcoat buttons, so as to fall nearly under one arm. This practice I have seen adopted since, and think if Johnny Gilpin had but taken this wise precaution he might have saved both hat and wig.

I was dreadfully fatigued with this day's travelling, being literally bruised black and blue. We suffered much inconvenience from the excessive heat of the day, and could well have dispensed with the company of two out of the four of our bulky companions.

We reached Prescott about five the same afternoon, where we met with good treatment at the inn; the female servants were all English, and seemed to vie with each other in attention to us. Here I was treated with a large tumbler of new milk by a Manx girl who was most kind to the English lads.

We saw little in the town of Prescott to interest or please. After an excellent breakfast we embarked on board the *Great Britain*, the finest steamer we had yet seen, and here we were joined by our new friends, to our great satisfaction.

At Brockville we arrived just in time to enjoy what was to me quite a novel sight—a ship-launch. A gay and exciting scene it was. The sun shone brilliantly on a concourse of people that thronged the shore in their holiday attire; the church bells rang merrily out, mingling with the music from the deck of this gaily painted vessel that, with flags and streamers, and a well-dressed company on board, was preparing for the launch.

To give additional effect, a salute was fired from a temporary fort erected for the occasion on a little rocky island in front of the town. The schooner took the water in fine style, as if eager to embrace the element which was henceforth to be subject to her. It was a moment of intense interest. The newly launched was greeted with three cheers from the company on board the *Great Britain*, with a salute from the little fort, and a merry peal from the bells, which were also rung in honour of a pretty bride that came on board with her bridegroom on their way to visit the falls of Niagara.

Brockville is just at the entrance of the Lake of the Thousand Islands, and presents a pretty appearance from the water. The town has improved rapidly, I am told, within the last few years, and is becoming a place of some importance.

The shores of the St Laurence assume a more rocky and picturesque aspect as you advance among its thousand islands, which present every variety of wood and rock. The steamer put in for a supply of fire-wood at a little village on the American side the river, where also we took on board five-and-twenty beautiful horses, which are to be exhibited at Cobourg and York (Toronto) for sale.

There was nothing at all worthy of observation in the American village, unless I except a novelty that rather amused me. Almost every house had a tiny wooden model of itself, about the bigness of a doll's house, stuck up in front of the roof or at the gable end. I was informed by a gentleman on board these baby-houses were for the swallows to build in.

It was midnight when we passed Kingston, so of course I saw nothing of that "key to the lakes." When I awoke in the morning the steamer was dashing gallantly along through the waters of the Ontario, and I experienced a slight sensation of sickness.

When the waters of the lake are at all agitated, as they sometimes are, by high winds, you might imagine yourself upon a tempest-tossed sea.

The shores of the Ontario are very fine, rising in waving lines of hill and dale, clothed with magnificent woods, or enlivened by patches of cultivated land and pretty dwellings. At ten o'clock we reached Cobourg.

Cobourg, at which place we are at present, is a neatly built